In memory of
Marilyn Peplow

First Published April 2012
© **Lifeware Publishing**
www.lifeware.co.uk

ISBN 978-1-4478-1132-9

For more information, please e-mail:
riseandstand@hotmail.co.uk

Cover art by: Dave & Mandy Scott-Morgan.

I WILL
RISE AND STAND

I have not scaled the heights to international fame;
Neither have I been swallowed up in the depths of addiction.
I am just an ordinary woman whose life
has been touched by God.

Acknowledgements

My thanks and gratitude to Yvonne Fairbairn, Kate Hayes, Sue Jones, Debbie Sale, Pam Sargent and Ann Parry, the girls of my home group, who suffered my trails and tribulations with me during the writing of this book.

My special thanks to Mandy Scott-Morgan, my closest friend and confidante who tirelessly proof read every line sometimes many times over when I failed to get it right. I couldn't have done it without you; you are worth your weight in rubies. To Dave, her husband, who inspired the title of the book; your music is fab. I love you both.

To Phil my husband and Lindsay my daughter, I never fail to give thanks for the blessing you have both been in my life. And thanks to all my friends who have believed in me, encouraged me and supported me in prayer.

Who would have thought over forty years ago sitting in a Church in Selly Oak Birmingham that the young lady sitting by me would one day write this book!

Sandie as she is known to her many friends was to most a fun loving girl who against all predictions left the big city and enrolled into Bible College, it was not an easy decision to make, yet this is the character of this wonderful lady.

Sandie in sharing her life story, not only portrays the important historic events of growing up in the post war years, but speaks out for the majority who never rise to the heights of stardom.

"I will Rise and Stand" takes us on a journey of fun, fear and frustration amongst the backdrop of the youth revaluation of the sixty's, to the present days of social and financial uncertainties.

Many reading this book will instantly identify with the issues of life from a standpoint of the majority, few tell their story, few take time to listen.

Sandie and her family are winners regardless of what some may think, I'm proud to call her a friend, you will be glad you read her story.

Rt Revd Dr David E Carr OSL
Bishop of Wroxall Abbey

Looking back over a long period of ministry, some characters stand out more than others; for all the good reasons, Sandie is one of those!

Sandie must have been a Christian for about two years when I first met her. In spite of her pre-Christian trials and struggles, described so graphically in this account, I remember Sandie being a young lady of enthusiasm, vitality and energy, always ready to be involved in the Lord's work. Sandie was also a fun-loving person, ably accompanied by lots of friends and noise!

As you will discover, this was a time in the life of the church *"when God turned up."* They were remarkable days and Sandie was deeply impacted by the Holy Spirit at that time. After all these years, Sandie has never lost her spiritual sparkle; she and her husband Phil, are still very much involved in the life and ministry of their local church.

For me it has been a great joy to have known Sandie and to have had a little involvement in her life. Whenever I see her now, we still end up talking about those exciting days!

I hope that you will not only be blessed, but also challenged, as you read this honest account of how God transformed the life of a young lady in such a marvellous way.

Rev. David Woodfield
Former Regional Superintendent, Elim North West Churches

Rise and Stand

Hey can I sing,
Of a wonderful thing
Of a beautiful mystery
Now in these days,
I am simply amazed at
WHAT THE GOOD LORD HAS DONE FOR ME.

And when I think of how,
I was lost in a crowd
Making my plans that never did work out,
I will rise and stand
And tell this land-
WHAT THE GOOD LORD HAS DONE FOR ME

Now I can say,
I'm a lifetime away,
From the person I used to be
Hey don't you know
Can't you see – don't it show
WHAT THE GOOD LORD HAS DONE FOR ME.

Cos when I think of it now,
I was lost in a crowd
But for the grace of God I'd be there now
So I'll rise and stand,
And tell this land –
WHAT THE GOOD LORD HAS DONE FOR ME.

© David Scott-Morgan

Chapters

Introduction

As dawn was breaking on the warm June morning, my thoughts meandered over the events that had brought me to this point in my life. I had cried myself to sleep the night before and the taste of the salty tears was still in my mouth as I emerged from sleep. The two strong arms of the man I loved pulled me closer when he realised I was awake. "Whatever did I do to make my dad hate me?" I sobbed.

"I love you," he whispered tenderly, as he kissed away my tears. Of all the many times he had said those words over the years that we had been together, never had they sounded so tender or held more emotion than they did now. Even in my despair, as I saw the fragile threads that had held me to my birth family dissolving, my heart soared. I felt gratitude and overwhelming love for this man lying beside me. People who knew me saw a vivacious, fun loving person, but he also knew the smouldering volcano that occasionally exploded into fits of temper. However, whatever I had thrown at him whether words, or in the early days the occasional missile, nothing phased this great oak of a man I had married over twenty years earlier. How I appreciated that quiet strength of his this day.

During a telephone conversation the evening before, my father told me he did not want to see me at what was possibly, my mother's deathbed. Not even from my earliest memories do I remember enjoying a harmonious relationship with him. He had vehemently hated not being able to control his self-willed offspring. Nevertheless, we later forged an uneasy truce when I became a Christian at the age of twenty-three. Over the years things even became quite amicable between us. I was therefore quite unprepared for the torrent of verbal abuse he had spewed at me down the telephone.

My mother had been rushed to the Intensive Care Unit at the Queen Elizabeth hospital in Birmingham where she now lay hovering between life and death. At this point the medical staff was still bewildered why every organ in her body had suddenly become totally paralysed. However, she was later diagnosed with the very rare and severely debilitating Guillan-Barrie syndrome.

While visiting my mother at the hospital the previous day, she had indicated to me through silent lips and pleading eyes the desire to see the son with whom both my parents had had no contact with for over six years, following a family argument. It was therefore with some trepidation I later telephoned my father to inform him I had taken my brother to visit my mother at the hospital. However I was shocked to hear him say it was not my brother's presence that was unwelcome at her bedside, but mine!

It appeared this unexpected tragedy had caused years of dormant rage my father had felt towards me to erupt. I stood transfixed; trembling in disbelief as I heard the sound of unleashed bitterness he had long felt towards me, coming down the telephone. Great teardrops fell from my chin as the years melted away and I was a teenager again. I felt again the pain of old wounds, as buried memories came surging to the surface of my mind.

As I lay in bed that morning, in my mind I traced God's hand through the many highs and lows I had experienced in my life and wondered where all this would eventually lead.

Chapter 1

In the beginning

I had heard many times of the difficulty my mother had giving birth to me on the morning of July 30th 1948. It may have been an omen, for I was to cause her much grief and anguish in the years that were to follow.

I was the first of the three children born to my Welsh father Alfred and my Birmingham born mother Irene. My earliest memories were of being about three years old. I was living with my parents in the back room of my Uncle Fred's house, who was my father's older brother. Also living in the house was my aunt Emily and my five cousins. My uncle and his family used the front living room and two of the three bedrooms. My aunt and mother shared the minute kitchen, which proved to be a recipe for disaster. Freddy and David were the oldest of my uncle's five children. The brothers aged around twelve and eleven respectively, shared a single bed in the tiny box room. Dyllis, the oldest of my uncle's three daughters, was a delicate child. Her straight, fair hair was as fine and wispy as her slender frame. Valmai, who was six, two years younger than Dyllis, was a friendly, independent child. She could usually be found sitting alone amusing herself with her toys on the front doorstep of the house and would happily talk to anyone who passed by. Susan was the chubby two-year-old baby of the family. Her strikingly beautiful, thick, dark, curly hair remained that way even into her adult years. Only eleven months younger than me we fought constantly, the cause of much friction between the adults. Nevertheless, our friendship remained, even when we outgrew childhood. The three girls also slept squeezed together, head to toe in a single bed placed at the foot of their parent's bed. My parents occupied the larger of the two back bedrooms. I continued to sleep in a cot wedged along side their bed until I was nearly five, because nothing bigger could be fitted into the room.

My parents were on the waiting list for a Council house. The deliberate overcrowding was thought to be a devious plan hatched by my uncle and my father to add points to my parents housing score, in order to for them to move up the list more quickly. Nevertheless it proved to be in vain because my parents still had to wait five long years before the Council offered them a house, by which time my parents had managed to save up enough money to put a deposit on a home of their own.

My uncle's pre-war semi-detached house was on Tessall Lane in Northfield, a suburb of Birmingham. Being a relatively new house it had the luxury of a bathroom, unlike many homes at that time. It also had a large rear garden, which later became home to a herd of pigs that were bred for slaughter. This was intended to be a moneymaking venture devised by the two Welsh brothers. In these early post war days any business that produced food was going to be profitable. Unfortunately, my uncle and my father spent most of their free time and all the profits from the business drinking in the King George V public house at the end of our road. Therefore, the business came to grief quite early on.

Relations between the two families became strained to breaking point over the years, mostly through arguments over the children. Although my mother was convinced her little girl could do no wrong, my cousins disliked me intensely because they were the recipients of my sly mischievous behaviour. I especially loved to torment my two eldest cousins by hiding their prized comics, bought each week with the wages from their newspaper rounds. My mother disregarded any of my cousins' complaints, increasing the feeling of irritation toward me.

My mother chose to lovingly use all her clothing coupons, still in operation from the war, to dress her only child the best that she was able. Unfortunately my aunt and uncle couldn't extend the same luxury to their brood of five children, although they both worked full time at the nearby Austin Motor Company. Unlike me, my impoverished cousins were mostly dressed in 'hand me down' clothes.

Another cause for resentment in the house was the lack of privacy. Having no lock on my parent's living room door or any of the cupboards they used my mother was convinced that her in-laws were pilfering her meagre food rations when she left the house, although she was never able to prove it.

*****

The two patriarchal brothers were brought up in poverty in South Wales. Their mother discovered she was pregnant with my uncle at the end of the First World War, soon after her sixteenth birthday. The only solution at this time to alleviate some of the stigma this shameful predicament caused was to be married as soon as possible, no matter how mismatched the couple were. By the time she was twenty, Adeline's marriage had produced three children. At this point her husband deserted her, leaving my grandmother to bring up the children, alone. To keep them out of an orphanage she did the only work available to her, which was to tramp around the streets of their hometown of Neath, selling clothes pegs on the doorsteps.

Adeline enjoyed a good time. As the children grew they were to know numerous 'uncles' who lived with them for a time before moving on. They were passed round to sympathetic members of their mother's family who took it in turns to look after these neglected children. It may have been their early adversity that caused my father and uncle to grow into hard, aggressive men who did not appreciate any sign of sensitivity in their children, regarding it as weakness.

All the children in the house were afraid of both men, especially when they returned home roaring drunk after a drinking session at the George V pub. For any misdemeanour the punishment was always a good hiding. The men were always quick to lash out for any wrong done by the children, whether justified or not. Among the offences I was punished for were bedwetting and stammering. When at the age of four, I took money from my mother's purse to buy sweets from the local shop, my father thought it fitting to use his belt to execute punishment for this heinous crime.

People found to their cost it was unwise to cross the infamous Welsh Lloyd brothers. One lazy, sunny Sunday afternoon, a neighbour complained to them about the noise all the children were making while playing outside in the street. For several weeks afterwards the Sunday afternoon noise also included the deafening roar of my uncle's motorbike constantly being revved up. The neighbours got the message and there were no more complaints about the children.

In the days before television occupied a place in nearly every home in the land, one of my great joys was to escape to the children's Saturday Matinee at the local Danillo picture house with my cousins. I shouted and screamed at the screen, along with all the other children from the neighbourhood. It was so exciting to be both terrified and thrilled by the latest episodes of Flash Gordon, Robin Hood and Sir Lancelot. We couldn't wait to go to the cinema the following week to see how our hero had managed to escape from the perilous situation he had found himself, in the final seconds of the previous episode.

Another great joy I had was going to Sunday school. Every parent and all the children in the area knew of Mr and Mrs MacRobbie who ran the Sunday school in their own home. Mr MacRobbie was a kindly jovial character, and was loved by all the children he taught. He had a broad Scottish accent and always wore a 'Dog Collar' with his black suit. The little hair he had was the same sandy colour as his freckles. Mrs MacRobbie on the other hand was a quiet Canadian lady, who always wore a navy blue felt hat that covered her fine, silver hair, which was always platted and tied neatly into a little bun at the back of her neck. She also wore a navy blue, calf length dress and coat with matching navy blue stockings and sensible navy blue shoes. Even in the comfort of their own home they did not relax their dress code while Sunday school was in progress.

Their three bed-roomed house had a large through-lounge; therefore both the front and back gardens could be viewed from the same large sitting room that doubled as the children's church. There would be several rows of miniature wooden chairs just big enough for the children to comfortably sit on set facing toward the front window, ready for us when we arrived. It was just like a grown-ups church.

Through my pre-school eyes Mr and Mrs MacRobbie looked very old indeed, and seemed very different from all the other grown ups I knew. They were very kind but firm, not allowing bad behaviour from any of the children. I loved everything about going to Sunday school. I enjoyed the stories about Jesus and the other people in the Bible. I loved drawing and colouring in the pictures of the stories we heard each week. I also loved clapping and singing the songs. Some of the songs had actions, which made us all laugh as we tried to copy the adults. Jolly Mr MacRobbie would play the accordion with gusto while Mrs MacRobbie would sit serenely playing the piano. I loved it when we were sometimes given sweets; sometimes they were for prizes, other times just for a treat before we went home. Above all the things at Sunday school, I loved Mr and Mrs MacRobbie the best.

Chapter 2

Growing pains

On a hot summer's day in 1953, my parents and I finally moved out of my Uncle Fred's house to live in our very own home. Accompanying us in the move was the latest addition to our family, my new baby sister Gail who had been born in the February of that year. The little three bed-roomed house my parents had bought was just up the hill on the opposite side of the road from my uncle's house. It was smaller having only one living room, unlike my uncle's two large sitting rooms. However it made up for this shortcoming by having a very spacious kitchen. The new garden was also very much smaller than the one we had left behind; nevertheless my parents were delighted with their new home. Compared to the severely cramped conditions they had endured for so long, the new little house seemed like a mansion to them. Having little furniture, the other grown ups and older children assisted my parents with the removal of their meagre belongings. Everyone was delighted that at last there would be extra space for all to live in. During the proceedings, dressed in my favourite yellow sundress, I played excitedly on the pavement outside our new house. I longed for someone I knew to come past so that I could tell them this was my very own house. Only my cousin Susan came but she just wanted to see what was going on, relieved that her archenemy was moving out at last.

Now that my father was removed from the constant influence of his brother, the years following the move became more stable than the turbulent time spent at my uncle's house. Free from the restrictions of living in lodgings, my father used his free time to renew the hobbies he had enjoyed in his youth.

A favourite pastime was rabbit hunting. Early every Sunday morning, it was his ritual to go off on his bike with his friend Billy Hopkins, scouring the local countryside for rabbits. The men refused to come home without at least one rabbit each for Sunday dinner. To aid them in this activity my father would take his two pet ferrets, Jack and Jill. They had been trained by my father not to kill the rabbits they had tracked down, but to leave that pleasure for the men.

When relatives and friends came to visit, after a few beers my father found great amusement in showing off the ferrets to his frightened guests. Knowing that most people thought they were vicious, he loved doing party tricks to demonstrate their tameness. My father would allow alcohol to dribble from his mouth, enticing a ferret to drink it from his chin. This was until the day one of the ferrets sank its needle sharp teeth into his lip, preferring the taste of my father's blood to the alcohol. Eventually, amid much commotion from the terrified audience, holding the animal between his knees he managed to prise open the vice like grip of the ferret and remove its teeth from his lip, fortunately with no serious damage being done. However, from that moment on my mother refused to allow the ferrets in the house. When thieves stole them from our back garden, my father was inconsolable. From that day on he stopped 'rabbiting' for without his beloved pets it wasn't the same anymore.

Pigeon racing became a later hobby. Fresh new wood shavings were required each week after cleaning out the pigeon loft. Unfortunately for me at nine years old I was given the job of collecting them from the local timber merchant every Saturday morning. The shavings formed a thick carpet under the large industrial saws. I would go crawling round under the machines with my large sack to collect my booty. The timber yard happened to be on the other side of Northfield from our house. Getting to the yard was no problem; sometimes I would even walk if it happened to be a nice day. The journey home however, was another matter. When the sack was full, it was nearly as high as I was. The buses were usually packed full of jostling Saturday shoppers who were not very happy to have the added inconvenience of a child spilling her huge sack of wood shavings all over their clothing, which happened quite frequently. Some of the conductors too, would get quite upset if I made a mess on the floor of their bus. However there were other more kindly conductors, who didn't seem to mind at all that shavings were spilled onto the floor of their bus. They would even help me to haul my sack on and off their vehicle. Sometimes I would stand for ages letting buses go past, just waiting for a bus to come along that was carrying a conductor I knew would be kind to me. My parents could never understand why there was so much inconsistency in the length of time the journeys took.

The pigeon races took place every Sunday during the summer months. The Saturday before the race, hundreds of racing pigeons would be transported in their baskets, by road and rail to the starting point. Very early on the Sunday morning the birds would be released simultaneously to fly to their individual homes. By early afternoon, they would begin to be seen in the sky by the waiting competitors. I would have already taken up my lookout position in the back garden where I was instructed to wait until the first pigeon appeared. When it came into view, I had to race into the house to inform my father who, more often than not, would be enjoying his Sunday afternoon nap. He would rush out into the garden covered in confusion and excitement, to grab the waiting seed tin which he would rattle with all his might in order to lure the hungry bird into the loft. Once the bird was in the shed, my father would put the bird's foot into a hole in the top of a purposely designed clock. Pressing a leaver would automatically register the time onto a reel of paper inside the machine. After the first pigeon arrived home I was gratefully released from duty, leaving my father to leisurely wait for the other birds to return home. Early in the evening he would go to the local pigeon fanciers club, where the steward would open each of the competitors' clocks, in order to establish who the regional winner was. My father would usually come home worse for drink, either having celebrated a victory or having consoled himself for losing the race. It was a joyous day for me when my father finally lost interest in this particular pastime.

There was never a time when my father was not consumed by one hobby or another, whether it was exhibiting canaries, wine making, or growing prize chrysanthemums. However, although his hobbies came and went, his enduring passion was his garden where he spent endless hours nurturing his beloved plants. Often he spent the entire day outside, coming into the house only to eat a meal. Summer or winter there was always some task that needed my father's attention.

Every July the sprawling motor manufacturer, where both my father and uncle were employed, closed down for two weeks. The majority of people living in the area also worked at the giant factory and most used this time to go on holiday. Therefore during this period the neighbourhood became like a ghost town.

My family always went on holiday with my uncle and his family of five children. Sometimes we were also joined by my father's sister, husband and their three children. When I was very young the families had tents, but later on we graduated to caravans. The general idea on these holidays was that the daytime was given over to the children, while the evenings were the adults' time to play. Every evening they would invade the nearest public house. I hated these nights because usually the children were required to loiter outside the pub. From time to time one of the adults would come out to see if we were all right, and to bribe us to behave with crisps and pop. Other times we were left back at the campsite to wait for them to come home. With no parental control quite often arguments between the children got out of control and fights sometimes broke out between the many cousins. I found out years later my mother hated these occasions as much as I did. Nevertheless she felt obliged to attend these nightly excursions to the local pub, even though she was aware of the contempt my father's family felt for her because she was teetotal.

I was only seven years old when, during one holiday, I was told to look after my two-year-old sister Gail, while they all went on their customary night out. Thinking she was asleep, Susan and I went to play on the swings in the park next door to the campsite. When we eventually returned to the tents, Gail was missing. Although Susan and I searched everywhere for her, she was nowhere to be seen. I became more and more distraught; petrified of the good hiding I would get from my father for leaving my little sister alone. Fortunately, seeing the grown ups return, a family from another tent on the site brought Gail back home, having found her wandering alone. I got into awful trouble but I didn't really understand the real gravity of the situation until many years later.

We were always on holiday when my birthday came round. It was always a fairly low-key affair because being at the seaside was a present in itself, I was told. Waking up in our caravan on my ninth birthday, I wondered what my parents had bought me for my special day. I imagined they were teasing me when it was not mentioned all through breakfast. However, by the time the meal was over I realised they were not teasing, and had forgotten this was my birthday. Only when my mother discovered me crying on my bed, did she remember. After telling our relatives in the surrounding caravans of the special occasion, she went to the camp shop to buy me a card and a present. There was activity in the other caravans as my aunts got quickly dressed in order to go over to the camp shop to also buy a gift for me. The shop mainly supplied buckets and spades, and fishing nets to catch tiddlers and crabs from the little rock pools at the beach, so there was only a small selection of items to choose from. My father was exasperated that the belated gifts and cards did little to cheer me up. I supposed it was because he was grown up that he didn't seem to understand how important birthdays are to a nine-year-old child, or why I felt so sad that no one had remembered my birthday.

During my childhood I was so prone to constant ear infections that I was finally admitted to hospital. My parents asked me to choose a special gift I would like to receive when I got home after my ordeal. It was an easy decision because I had seen a doll I particularly admired on display in the window of a local toyshop. Every time I went past the shop I would look longingly at her, never imagining she could ever be mine. When in great anticipation I arrived home from the hospital I was told the doll had been far too expensive, instead I was presented with a ball of green wool, a pair of knitting needles and a knitting pattern. As knitting was mother's passion she couldn't understand why I was not delighted to have this substitute gift. This crushing blow quenched any smouldering desire I may have had to also take up her much-loved hobby. I was learning fast that life was strewn with disappointment.

The birth of my baby brother, who was born at home, was an unforgettable memory of my childhood. My sister and I woke one Sunday morning to hear unfamiliar noises in the house. Going downstairs to investigate, I found a friendly oriental nurse in our kitchen who was boiling towels on the gas stove. The air was full of tension and my mother was nowhere to be seen. I had never seen my father in such a state of panic. He nervously told Gail and me that we were going to spend the day with a neighbouring family (whose children were of a similar age to my sister and me) and that we were soon to have a new baby.

Gail and I arrived home later that day, bursting to tell our parents all about the wonderful time we'd had, picnicking at a park, where there had been swings, slides and lots of other things to play on. However, we were stopped in our tracks because my father had an announcement of his own to make. Gail and I were immediately taken upstairs to see the baby boy that had been born to my mother in our absence. When my mother told us the new baby's name was to be Bryn I was horrified having never heard the name before. I was told my father chose the name because it was Welsh, to honour the 'land of his fathers'.

For days the house was never empty of people, all billing and cooing over the new baby. As one person left, another arrived, everyone chattering and laughing. Happiest of all was my father; this event was like a thousand Christmases rolled into one for him. I had no way of knowing how much, or for how long he had longed for a son. He could now proudly boast to his siblings that his branch of the family tree also had a son to carry on the family name. My nine-year-old mind didn't quite understand why the event generated so much excitement. I didn't know either how much my life was to change because of my father's unabashed adoration of my new sibling.

As I grew toward my teenage years the fear I had once felt for my father was replaced by hatred. Coming home drunk after his lunchtime drinking sessions at the local King George V pub with his brother, each Sunday afternoon he would sleep off the effects in his armchair by the fireside. I hated these Sunday afternoons because he was so unpredictable when he awoke. My sister, brother and I would be as quiet as church mice, fearing to wake him up before he had had his full sleep, knowing how volatile he could become if his Sunday afternoon nap were disturbed. Sometimes he would emerge from his sleep in a playful mood, wanting to wrestle with one of us. It was usually Bryn who would fearlessly take up the challenge, after Gail and I had fled from the room. Invariably the episode ended in tears when Bryn was hurt. Occasionally it was my father who was hurt when Bryn managed to land a lucky blow. If my brother cried during one of these wrestling matches my father's playful mood would quickly change to anger, believing Bryn was crying for nothing. In his inebriated state he was not aware of his strength. Once when I happened to be the recipient of one of these Sunday afternoon play-wrestling matches, he crushed my toes in his hands so vigorously I could not catch my breath to tell him how much pain I was in. When he saw my tears he just waved me away, tired of the game.

From time to time he would wake up from his Sunday afternoon stupor in a maudlin mood, keen to reminisce about his wartime experiences. Sometimes, when he began telling me stories of the war, Gail would mischievously sit on the floor behind his chair outside his line of vision. She would wickedly attempt to make me laugh, by making exaggerated facial expressions in mock agreement with whatever he was saying, to get me into trouble! This was because we knew how quickly his mood could change, but we had become so used to his outbursts of rage they ceased to hold any threat for us; instead he had become an object of derision and scorn.

Chapter 3

A seed of hope

I loved learning and my happiest memories, until the age of ten, were of being at school. While reading a story to the class on Friday afternoons, my teacher would occasionally call out my name and ask me to spell a particularly difficult word from the story, one of several that she had coached me to memorise, at my request. It made me feel very proud when the class gasped at my knowledge.

Having already done quite well at school, I believed the promise my father made to me at the beginning of year five, that he would buy me a brand new bike if I came first in the end of year exams. Therefore I worked extra hard in order to achieve the promised reward. When, at the end of the year, I proudly handed him my report that stated I was top of the class, he laughingly told me he didn't remember making any such promise to me.

The crushing disappointment I felt, paled into insignificance when my kindly class teacher Miss Large, informed me I was to move up to a higher class at the beginning of the new school year as another reward for my achievement. I was horrified! Not only did I have to leave all my friends, worse still, the class teacher was none other than the formidable Mrs Brownley who struck fear into the heart of every child in the school. To hear your name called out by her in the school corridor, caused not only feet to stop moving immediately but your heart also, because a public and humiliating lashing from her very sharp tongue usually followed.

A feeling of dread steadily grew in me during the summer holidays at the thought of going into Mrs Brownley's class, until I was overwhelmed by it. However, a great idea came to my mind, I resolved I would not go into her class; I would kill myself instead. At this moment the thought of dying appealed to me much more than having to spend a year being taught by the fearsome Mrs Brownley. Whether the stories of heaven I had once heard in Sunday school were buried somewhere deep in my subconscious I don't know, but I had no fear of what lay on the other side of the grave whatsoever. I imagined whatever being dead was like couldn't be any worse than being in Mrs Brownley's class for a whole year.

My mother had frequently warned me not to touch a large mole I had on my back because if I did I would probably bleed to death. I had shared a bedroom with my little sister since our baby brother arrived, so I waited until I was sure she was asleep, then I scratched and scratched at the mole until my fingers felt sticky and knew I had succeeded in making it bleed. That night I thought nervously to myself, "Well this is it! I'm now going to die." I was sad to be leaving my parents behind, but relieved I would not now be taught by that awful teacher. "Goodbye world, goodbye Mrs Brownley, you won't be seeing me next term!" I thought smugly. I pondered on what being dead was going to be like as I drifted off into oblivion.

The next thing I knew, bright sunlight was streaming into the room as my mother opened the bedroom curtains. As usual she told Gail and me it was time to get up for school. I was bitterly disappointed that I was not dead and not going to escape Mrs Brownley's class after all. While getting dressed my mother saw that my vest was covered in blood. She fiercely interrogated me over the cause but I didn't tell her why my mole had bled so much. It was my secret.

That September I went into the new class. I made new friends quite quickly, so the upheaval wasn't quite as difficult as I had imagined. However, Mrs Brownley was every bit as frightening as I had anticipated. The name fitted her perfectly for it was so descriptive of her. Her sombre dress invariably consisted of tweed skirts and knitted twin sets, always in varying tones of brown, grey or beige. Her silver laced dark brown hair was tied into a big bun that sat neatly at the nape of her neck. Added to that, the round silver rimmed glasses perched on the end of her large bulbous nose made her a very daunting presence. We later discovered that if she believed someone was misbehaving in any way, she would look slowly around the class, her thin lips pursed tightly together looking for the culprit. Everyone hoped it would not be them her dark brown, hawk like eyes would finally rest upon, because of the retribution it would bring to that individual. On one occasion her eyes stopped at a scrawny little boy called Dennis Eccleshaw. She called him out to the front of the class and made him stand on the nature table; this was so that everyone could see him clearly. She then set about commenting on his scruffy and unkempt appearance, drawing particular attention to his dirty, unwashed knees. All eyes were fixed on any object in the room rather than on him, knowing that anyone of us could be subject to this degrading exhibition.

I too, had my own humiliation at her hands. It came on a day when I happened to be engrossed in conversation with my friend sitting next to me. As Mrs Brownley walked round the classroom I hadn't noticed her quietly walk up the aisle behind me. She stood over me, waiting for me to notice her. When I did, I was dragged from my seat to the front of the class, where she mercilessly slapped my legs for not paying attention. It became a battle of wills. Had I cried, she may have taken pity on me and stopped. But my pride would not allow me to give any one the satisfaction of seeing they had reduced me to tears. Although my legs were red and stinging, I returned to my seat in triumph, having managed to successfully hold back the tears that were ready to cascade down my face.

However, during this unhappy year a rainbow appeared

every Friday afternoon during the last hour of school. We were told to put our tools away, lay our heads on our folded arms and listen to the latest chapter of the book Mrs Brownley was currently reading to us. She chose wonderful stories that set our imaginations ablaze as we were transported to exciting places in our minds. My favourite story was John Bunyan's 'Pilgrim's Progress.' I was impatient for Friday to come round each week, eager to hear about Pilgrim's adventures after he left his home in the City of Destruction to head toward the Celestial City. I loved to hear about the many trials and tribulations he encountered on the journey. Whatever traps or detour his wily adversaries used to frustrate his efforts to get to his destination, his resolve never weakened because he could always see the shimmering light of the city in the distance with his eye of faith. I imagined it must be a wonderful place for it was the place where there was no more death, nor sorrow or crying and there was no more pain, for the former things had passed away 'Revelation chapter 21 verse 4'. I was so sad when the story ended.

It was around this time that my mother, out doing her weekly shopping, encountered Mrs MacRobbie my old Sunday school teacher. Having not seen each other for a number of years Mrs MacRobbie told my mother the Pillar of Fire Sunday school was finally leaving its home in her house to relocate to a purpose-built church that was in the process of being erected on the brand new Council estate at the top of our road. The MacRobbies would also move to live in the flat above the church. Because I had previously attended the Sunday school, she asked my mother to invite me to the forth-coming grand opening of the new church. Being so kind to me in the past, I felt obliged to accept her invitation. I was also curious to see inside the building.

The music and singing brought back happy memories of the times I had spent at Sunday school in Mrs MacRobbies former home. Therefore, I happily agreed when Mr

MacRobbie invited me to return to the service the following week. I also went the week after, and the week after that, until going to Sunday school became part of my weekly routine again.

Mr and Mrs MacRobbie had acquired a co-worker called Mrs Andrews who had taken over the organ playing from Mrs MacRobbie. She also taught the older children, when the Sunday school dispersed into their separate classes. Her prim hairstyle and old-fashioned style of dress concealed the fun loving person beneath. Mrs Andrews was blessed with the ability to make the lessons fun and entertaining. Kindness radiated from her twinkling eyes causing us to feel ashamed when we gave her cause to reprimand us. I had the privilege of spending extra time with this delightful lady because she had to walk past my house on the way to her bus stop. As we walked down the hill together, each week she would tell me about Jesus and seemed to love Him as much as Mr and Mrs MacRobbie did. One Sunday, before we left church, I told Mrs Andrews that I too wanted to know Jesus like she did. So she sat with me on the stairs of the Sunday school where I invited Jesus to come into my life. Walking down the hill towards home I understood how Christian felt in the book 'The Pilgrim's Progress' when he had gazed at the cross and his burdens rolled away, for I felt as if I walked on air.

People very quickly saw a difference in me because I was so happy. I went to Mrs MacRobbies' church at every opportunity. No attempt at ridicule by my friends or family could dampen my new found faith. Therefore, the mockery dwindled to friendly light-hearted banter when they realised my mind could not be changed. Nevertheless, when the excitement I felt in knowing that Jesus was real slowly faded, with it went my enthusiasm to go to church. Increasingly I began to miss meetings, as it became easier and easier to stay away. Finally, while we were walking home from church one Sunday, with some trepidation I told Mrs Andrews I would not be coming back to church again, for I was no longer a Christian. Totally unfazed by this information, Mrs Andrews robustly declared, "Oh, you'll be back my dear! Maybe you will be a mother or even a grandmother, but you will be back. Take my word! Jesus does not take His hand off a person's life once He has put it on." I wanted to cry for I felt I didn't deserve her kindness. I didn't believe what she said either. The feelings of grief and guilt I subsequently felt because I had walked away from God eventually subsided and the sharp pangs of remorse that stabbed me whenever I unexpectedly heard a favourite hymn on the radio or television also faded in time.

I changed schools completely after I left Mrs Brownley's class for it was time to move up to senior school. Like most of the children in the area who had not passed the 11plus exam and graduated to grammar school, I went to the local secondary school. I soon settled down to my new environment and happily made new friends from the numerous pupils who had come from the many different junior schools scattered around the area. Memories of my previous school, both good and bad, eventually became a distant blur.

However, it was an ill-fated day when I discovered how easy it was to make the other pupils in the class laugh, simply by clowning around. Because it won me popularity my behaviour and desire to achieve gradually spiralled downward. Over the next four academic years I grew increasingly disruptive and therefore spent many hours loitering in the corridor, having been thrown out of the classroom for bad behaviour by exasperated teachers. Approval from my peers became far more important than attaining good grades. I hated authority and became more and more rebellious toward any teacher who tried to enforce discipline upon me. I didn't realise how much the teachers returned my feelings for them until I saw my all-important school leaving report. My class teacher refused to write anything good about me, he wrote, "Sandra has no interest in the school or anything it stands for. She just sits daydreaming all day. Prospects for her future are very poor". When pupils showed each other their glowing reports I made a great show of bravado, so that no one saw how humiliated I felt by mine. When, at the age of fifteen, I walked out of the school gates for the last time, I was euphoric as I walked to freedom and to my future.

Chapter 4

Learning to fly

I started work on the first Monday morning of August 1963 soon after my fifteenth birthday. I had secured the post of Office Junior in the factory control office at the Kalamazoo, a small paper-printing factory about twenty minutes walk from my house. It was really mother's excellent reputation at the company for being a diligent, reliable worker that secured me the post that had become vacant. She had been employed there as a cleaner for several years. My mother was delighted when I succeeded in getting the job, having been greatly concerned that my poor school leaving report may have jeopardised any chance of getting a job at all. I felt very proud of getting an 'office job', for most of my friends only attained work in the local shops or factories.

My hands were hot and clammy as I perched nervously on the edge of my seat, in the personnel department on my first morning, waiting for someone to take me to the area where I would work. After a short time, a girl walked into the office, fashionably dressed in a mini skirt and matching top. Her deep raspberry colour hair, courtesy of the local chemist shop, was neatly cut into the latest mod style. She told me her name was Sue and she had come to escort me to the factory control office. We chattered easily as we walked through the labyrinth of corridors toward the factory office. I had immediately warmed to her so was pleased when she told me we would be working together. The post I was about to take up was the one Sue had just vacated. She told me she had been promoted because a member of staff had recently retired. When we arrived at our destination I was literally trembling with fright. Sue introduced me to Ted Samuels, my boss, who was the foreman over the whole printing department that surrounded the little factory control office where I would be working. I could feel the eyes of everyone in the room peering at me as Sue led me around the office, introducing me to each of the twelve men and women who would be my colleagues.

Sue and I discovered we lived quite close to each other. We soon became the best of friends and even spent most of our free time together. She enjoyed introducing me to my first taste of local nightlife, taking me to the enormously popular dances at the Black Horse pub, a large black and white eighteenth century coaching house set in the heart of Northfield, and the Bournbrook pub, a run down pub a further few miles away. Crowds of teenagers would throng to these popular places at weekends. The dances were held in the dimly lit little upstairs function rooms that were also sometimes hired out for wedding receptions. As the evenings wore on, the overpowering smell of beer mingled with cigarette smoke would fill the air. Standing in one place for too long was unwise, because your feet could become fixed to the sticky wooden floor where beer spilled from the tiny tables that had been crammed with beer bottles and glasses in the overcrowded dance halls. In these rather seedy places it was difficult to hold a conversation because of the deafening music coming from the tiny stage, where the live bands played. Little did we know at the time, that some of these amateur groups would go on to gain great professional success.

I found that going to work was much more enjoyable than going to school; the main reason was my friendship with Sue Jones. I often stayed at her house at the weekends. I shared Sue's single bed, where we would usually gossip and giggle for most of the night. Sue's dad would bring us tea and toast to eat in bed in the morning, which I thought was a wonderful treat.

The first time I slept at Sue's I unwisely wore my prized slimming garment that I always slept in at home. It was an aid to weight loss, my continual project. The garment consisted of a pair of plastic pantaloons that were worn over pyjamas, causing the wearer to sweat profusely. I hadn't realised that wearing my pantaloons while sleeping in Sue's bed would cause her to perspire too. We woke in the middle of the night to find we were lying in a river of sweat, even our hair was ringing wet. Fortunately we didn't wake the rest of the household with our giggling, as we changed our drenched nightwear and bedclothes.

I adored Sue's parents, even though Sue's mum initially scared me because she could be quite fierce. However, I found she was really quite soft when we became better acquainted. Sue's dad was very sweet and good-humoured. I went to Sue's house at every given opportunity because I was made very welcome, and the atmosphere seemed so much more relaxed than at my home.

During our tea breaks at work, Sue and I sometimes spoke about our aspirations and dreams for the future. Like many teenagers, we imagined how exciting it would be to be famous and imagined how we might meet the Beatles, who had just exploded onto the pop scene like a meteor. Sue and I were besotted by them, and had pictures of the Fab Four plastered all over the walls around our desks in the office, which greatly amused the older members of staff. My bedroom walls at home were also covered with their pictures. Sue and I were inconsolable at not being able to get tickets to see the Beatles when they came to perform at the Birmingham Hippodrome. The tickets had been sold out immediately they came on sale; however we refused to be deterred. We thought that if we hung around the stage door until the Beatles arrived for their concert, we might catch a glimpse of them. So we caught a bus to town very early in the morning on the day they were due to appear at the Hippodrome in Birmingham, prepared to wait all day to see them, if necessary. However, when we arrived we were horrified to see hoards of teenage girls, who apparently had the same idea as we did. When the Beatles eventually arrived, camouflaged in a police van, there was a huge stampede toward the vehicle, everyone hoping to get a glimpse before the Fab Four disappeared into the building. Sue's handbag was broken and I lost one of my stilettos in the crush. Nevertheless, I didn't mind having to hobble home shoeless, because it had been great fun, even though we didn't get to see the 'Fab Four 'after all. My parents were both desperately worried about my latest mania. When the Beatles came on the television one night I screamed at the screen. For once my father kept quiet because he had no idea how to handle the situation, fearing I had totally gone off my head. My mother on the other hand, threatened to take me to the doctor, which always meant she was at a loss to know what else to do with me.

When the Kalamazoo introduced a new system of work in the factory, I was asked to be the first clerk to work on this important new enterprise. Many thought I was throwing away a great opportunity to further my career when I refused to accept the post. Having been employed by the firm for less than a year I had become bored and restless and wanted excitement elsewhere.

My father suggested I join my cousin Christine, who was working as a waitress in a hotel at Great Yarmouth on the east coast for the summer season. Her friend had returned home, leaving my cousin to work there alone. My father imagined his favourite niece might be a good influence on me, and thought perhaps working away from home for a short period, may cause me to become more settled. I was delighted at the suggestion and eagerly agreed to join my cousin. After a number of excited phone calls to Great Yarmouth, to confirm my cousin's employers were happy to engage me, I was on my way.

I was sad saying goodbye to friends, colleagues, Sue and her family. Nevertheless the excitement and expectation I felt about this adventure outweighed any misgivings I may have privately harboured about the move. It was two months before my sixteenth birthday that I travelled by coach to Great Yarmouth, where I would begin working as a waitress, alongside my cousin Christine. My mother was dismayed that I had thrown away good career prospects at the Kalamazoo and that I had chosen to live away from home.

A few hours after I set off, I could see my cousin Christine smiling at me as I nervously stepped off the coach in Great Yarmouth's coach station. She had the demeanour of a woman older than her seventeen years, and was aware of her sultry good looks. Her long dark wavy hair danced rhythmically on her shoulders to the melodious clink, clink of her stiletto heels, as she walked across the concrete floor to greet me. She oozed confidence, having grown up in and around the public houses in Birmingham that her parents had managed.

After we had said our hellos we were on our way to the small family run Elsfred Hotel. Christine took me to the attic where we were to sleep. Although the décor was a bit old fashioned, the room was quite cosy and I loved the way the ceiling came down nearly to the floor at one end of the room. Our room was so high up it seemed as if we could see all of Great Yarmouth from our little window. We could also see what was hidden from the many holidaymakers that came to Great Yarmouth, the dark, dingy back yards of the surrounding hotels which were in stark contrast to the delightfully decorated hotel frontages. Hanging baskets and flower tubs adorned every nook and cranny available. The hotels used them in competition with each other to arrest the senses of the passing holidaymakers, in order to lure possible clientele into the hotel.

I enjoyed living on the premises, only having to run down stairs to be at work. The people frequenting our hotel were mainly families but Christine and I were delighted to welcome the occasional single parties too. Most of the guests were in buoyant holiday mood, eager to have a good time, we became so fond of some, it was sad to wave goodbye when they came to the end of their holiday.

Great Yarmouth received a clear signal from the new pirate radio station Radio Caroline, illegally broadcasting from a boat anchored near the local coastline. While Christine and I laid tables during the day the ship's continual, contemporary, pop music could be heard throughout the hotel. The combination of sunny weather, music, and happy holidaymakers was a delightful heady mixture making the summer of 1964 a very happy new experience.

Unlike Christine, I wasn't a very good waitress. Trying to carry as many plates as my experienced cousin caused me to regularly drop them. Occasionally I even managed to drop food into the laps of the diners. Nevertheless, the holidaymakers were very kind to me and some were even amused by my mishaps, unlike the proprietors Mr and Mrs Evans, whose irritation at my incompetence steadily grew.

Our employers' three grown-up sons also lived in the hotel. Christine and I didn't see very much of the two older brothers because they had no interest in the hotel and spent very little time there. The only son who bothered with Christine and me was happy-go-lucky Brian. He was twenty-one and unemployed. Whenever Brian was around the hotel, he would either be looking in the mirror making sure his Teddy-Boy quiff was still looking good, or flirting with Christine. When he wasn't in the hotel, he was at the American Air Force base situated near Great Yarmouth, because many of his friends were stationed there. When the bar in the hotel was closed to clientele, Brian would sometimes fill it with uniformed Americans. One Sunday afternoon, finding Christine and me watching television in his parents lounge, Brian invited us to join his friends. Christine jumped at this chance to socialise with the Americans, and rose wonderfully to the occasion. She charmed them with her wit and geniality. I on the other hand, being only sixteen, was mortified by the experience and sat on my bar stool unable to speak. The Americans attempted to include me in their conversation, but I went crimson when anyone spoke to me, so one by one they ceased trying to include me. I was so glad when this ordeal came to an end. I hadn't realised how obvious my discomfort was, until my cousin later berated me for embarrassing her.

When we were children, the only time Christine and I met was during the holidays or on occasional family visits. Living and working together made us realise how very little we had in common. I became increasingly lonely and desperately homesick. Christine wasn't ready to return home so she suggested we find employment at a different hotel, thinking a change of scenery may make me feel happier. After some persuasion I reluctantly agreed, although what I really wanted was to go home. I told my mother of our plans to look for work elsewhere, during our weekly telephone call. The telephone was situated in the basement, just outside our employer's living quarters. I had not been aware that my employers, who always had their living room door slightly ajar, were listening and could hear everything I said.

When we started work the next day we were told our employment was to be terminated at the end of the week. Relations between our employers, my cousin and me had become increasingly tense due to Christine's flirting with their son and my inability to wait on tables. Therefore overhearing that we intended to leave gave them a good reason to dismiss us. I was horrified at the news, and felt so ashamed that I wanted to die. Not only did I get myself the sack, but my cousin too!

Christine and I were silently lost in our own thoughts, as we travelled back to Birmingham. My appetite for excitement had totally evaporated; I just wanted to go home. My big adventure had ended in humiliation and disgrace. To my surprise both my parents had been supportive about the news of my sacking, and had kindly urged me to come home. Nevertheless, I had mixed feelings about returning home. I could hardly wait to see my family again, but during the last few months I had loved being free from the restrictions of parental control. A feeling of dread descended on me as I neared my journey's end.

Chapter 5

Into the storm

Seeing my parents standing on the platform of Digbeth coach station as the bus came back into Birmingham, brought me to tears as I realised how much I had missed them. Safe in the bosom of my family again, the humiliating events I experienced at Great Yarmouth that led to this moment seemed like a million miles away.

The hope that my father had previously had, that my leaving home for a short time might cause me to settle down, had been a vain one. Initially he and I tried hard not to argue as we had before I went away, but very soon the cracks in our relationship began to show. My father was determined I would not flout his authority, and I felt more restless than ever. It was not long before the rows began again as our relationship deteriorated to an all time low. The arguments were invariably followed by literally months of silence between us, which was preferable to me.

Unfortunately, I loved a good discussion and was very opinionated. I would even play devil's advocate just for the fun of the debate. A discussion with my father usually ended when he flew into a rage, believing my difference of opinion was insolence and defiance of his authority. Having differing opinions on almost everything, we learned to say very little to each other. Nevertheless, there were occasions when we would unintentionally ramble into a conversation about some current political situation, or an article one of us may have read in a current newspaper. Before I knew it, my father would jump up from his chair, stomp out of the room shouting what an arrogant, know-all bastard I was, as doors were slammed in his wake. I would be left reeling, wondering what it was I had said to upset him so much.

Unlike me, my sister Gail enjoyed a close relationship with our father, which I envied. They laughed at the same things and she genuinely agreed with most of his opinions. Like everyone else my dad was won over by Gail's amiable charm. Before she would ask him for anything, first she would sit on the arm of his chair and gently stroke his hair while laughingly telling him how wonderful he was. He knew this was just an ambush to get what she wanted but he didn't mind. They would usually both end up laughing and more often than not my father happily complied with her wishes. They both knew he was putty in my sister's hands, but he didn't mind.

Following one of my rows with my father I clumsily attempted to copy one of my sister's manoeuvres on him with disastrous results. Gail had once put a letter in the lunch box in which he used to take his sandwiches to work. Apparently it told how wonderful she thought he was. My mother shared with me how amused my father had been by this childish show of affection. So in an attempt to stop the inevitable prolonged silent treatment that always followed a row, I decided to follow Gail's example and put a note in his lunch box. Pouring out my heart in an unprecedented way, I boldly told him that I still loved him even though I disagreed with his opinions. I was full of anticipation as I watched him go off to do the night shift at the factory, knowing he was carrying my note to work. Drifting off to sleep that night, I hoped he would be pleased when he opened his lunchbox to find my letter, and that it may help to cement our relationship a little.

My father's daily ritual when he came home from the nightshift was to take a cup of tea up to my mother who would still be in bed. Following a brief conversation, they would exchange places; my mother leaving my father snuggled up in the warm bed to come downstairs to start the day. I was sure they must have discussed my letter, so I was eager to hear what my father had said about it. I waited patiently for my mother to open the subject while we sat in the living room, eating our usual breakfast of tea and toast by the fireside. Eventually my mother remarked, "Your father's furious with you," I was shocked into silence by her words, but eventually said "Why?!" "Because of that silly note you put in his lunch box, he thinks you were laughing at him." she said calmly. I felt angry and ridiculous that my attempts at reconciliation were so misconstrued. Following a short, fairly heated exchange of words, the matter was never mentioned again by anyone. However, I determined I would never allow myself to be vulnerable with anyone in the family ever again.

I hadn't realised that I was sacrificing my valued friendship with Sue Jones by going away for the summer. Understandably being a teenager who liked the nightlife, Sue hadn't stayed at home waiting for me to return. The girl, who filled my post at the Kalamazoo, had also filled my shoes as Sue's best friend and had been introduced to all the pubs and clubs where Sue and I had had so much fun together. Although they invited me to go with them I found that three was a crowd. Now being the outsider, my friendship with Sue gradually came to an end. I sorely missed the oasis her family had been to me when things became too much to bear at home. I felt very lonely, and slowly descended into a pit of self-pitying despair.

One Saturday morning I was again going through the usual ritual of being ignored by my family over some minor dispute. Gail was still in bed and my parents were out doing their weekly shopping with my little brother in tow. I sat gloomily alone in the living room, listening to the voices inside my head telling me how worthless I was, and that my life would never change. I did not want to live any longer, so for a second time I decided to put an end to it all. I went into the kitchen and carefully closed the windows and doors, then turned on the gas cooker. When I had finally positioned myself comfortably on the floor I put my head inside the oven. After sitting there for about fifteen minutes, I was surprised to find that I didn't even feel tired. I thought I would have just peacefully drifted off into oblivion, never to wake up. However I felt really nauseous from the dreadful smell of the gas, and my back ached from the awkward position I was lying in. I realised maybe I didn't want to commit suicide after all. I certainly did not want to be found dead in a pool of vomit, which would have been the case had I stayed there for much longer. At this point my sister, who was also not speaking to me, appeared in the doorway.

"What on earth are you doing?" she shrieked,

"What does it look like?" I snapped back.

Looking out of the kitchen window, in an attempt to abort my now redundant suicide bid, Gail told me that she could see our father coming up the garden path. In a state of blind panic, we flung all the doors and windows open, then ran round the living room and kitchen waving newspapers in the air, in an attempt to get rid of the smell of gas. Eventually we collapsed onto the settee in a fit of giggles. At least I now had one friend in the family.

When our parents did finally arrive, smelling the gas as he walked through the door, our father roared in anger. He wanted to know which idiot had been playing around with the cooker, knowing the house could possibly blow up at any second. Because he wasn't speaking to me, thankfully it was Gail who received the full force of his fury.

The situation at home continued in much the same vein. I decided a less dramatic solution to my plight than suicide, would be just to leave home. I scanned the ads in the flats to let column of the Birmingham Evening Mail, and eventually had a meeting with a twenty-one year old secretary needing someone to share the running costs of her one-bedroom flat. As we seemed to hit it off immediately, I agreed to move into the roomy first floor apartment.

The flat was in a very large three-storey Victorian house that had been converted into flats. Situated in an inner city district of Birmingham, far from where I was currently living with my parents. I was seventeen and an office junior, so I earned much less money than my flatmate, therefore she kindly allowed me to make a much lower contribution to the running of the place than she did. Nevertheless there was still very little left of my wages after I had paid my part of the bills.

The firm I worked for was a small, family run business, which was a short bus ride from my parents' house. However, from my new address it was two long bus journeys. With nearly all my wages spent on the flat's rent and running costs plus the costly bus fares, there was barely anything left for food, and nothing for luxuries. The five women I worked with in the small office, understanding my difficult circumstances, took pity on me. Every week they brought groceries into work for me, telling me different stories of how they had unintentionally bought too much food when doing their weekly shop. Even Helen, a pensioner who worked only a few hours a week, would bring tins of food in for me. They acted as if I was doing them a favour by taking it off their hands. I felt terribly indebted to them for their heart-warming generosity.

Heather, my flat mate, was very accomplished. She was a first-rate cook and also made most of her own clothes, she appeared to excel at whatever she put her hand to. Her numerous talents made me feel quite inferior and inept by comparison. She was popular and having a lot of friends, meant she went out a great deal. Unfortunately, her active social life meant I was left alone in the flat for much of the time. Sometimes I would lie awake until 3 or 4 o'clock in the morning, waiting to hear her return. I became increasingly nervous in the eerie, shadowy rooms of the flat and was easily frightened when I heard noises coming from the surrounding flats, or when I heard the ghostly, howling wind rustling through the trees in the gardens below.

Alone one night, as usual I couldn't sleep and lay awake until the early hours of the morning, waiting for Heather to come home, when I thought I saw a ghost standing outside the bedroom window. It had no head or legs, just what looked like a naked torso. I was too frightened to even reach up to pull the overhead chord, which turned the light off. From time to time I would dare to take another peep. It was still there, silently taunting me. Afraid even to move I put my head under the blankets and stayed as still as I could, until I finally fell asleep.

When I woke up the next morning, I noticed Heather's pink sweater draped over the fireplace in our bedroom to dry. I was so relieved when I realised my ghoulish apparition had been nothing more than the reflection of the sweater on the window.

I realised living at home, even with all the rows, was better than living like this. The novelty of being able to have a bath at one o'clock in the morning was short lived. Knowing no-one was there to care what time I took a bath made it a very hollow victory. After what seemed like an endless winter of misery, I gratefully accepted when my father took pity on me and invited me to return home.

The other teenager working in the office was Joy, whose contribution to my lonely plight was her friendship. I gladly accepted the kind invitation to join her and her sister when they went on their regular Tuesday night excursion to dance at the local Chalet Country Club.

Joy was very different to me in every way. She was quiet and dignified. Even her dress code was quiet, dignified and understated. Joy described her sister in glowing terms but I was still a little apprehensive about meeting her, afraid she might think I was intruding on the sisters' night out. However I needn't have worried, for there was an instant rapport between us. My first impression of Lorraine was how different she was from her younger sister. She was smaller and much darker than Joy and wore very trendy clothes. Her thick dark hair, cut into the latest Mary Quant style, made her enormous dark brown eyes look even larger than they really were. She was very friendly and laughed easily. By the end of the evening, a deep friendship had been formed between us.

Disappointingly I found the Chalet Country Club rather grim. Although some really good bands played there, only the same faithful few people turned up each week to hear them. Nonetheless, I was glad I was able to escape from the confines of my home for one night of the week, at least.

When Lorraine asked me if I cared to join her on a visit to her grandmother, I was delighted, having been told that she entertained her guests by telling their fortunes using playing cards. All forms of fortune telling fascinated me so I really hoped Lorraine's gran might read the cards for me. During our visit I sat waiting in eager anticipation. Eventually, just as Lorraine had predicted, after the tea and cakes were finished, out came the playing cards. I was captivated, and found it amazing that the cards were able to tell Lorraine's grandmother things about my family that were impossible for this stranger to have knowledge of.

I went to have my cards read by Lorraine's grandmother countless times after this initial introduction, for enough predictions came true to entice me back to see her again and again.

Chapter 6

She's leaving home

While I was growing up, my uncle Fred and his family had moved house. They conveniently moved to the house right next door to the King George V pub, my uncle's favourite drinking haunt. Following the move, he had spent an increasing amount of time inside the pub, since he didn't have so far to stagger home when its doors finally closed at the end of the night. Having resigned herself to her husband's way of life, my aunt Emily would frequently join her husband, also becoming a regular at the pub.

By 1967 my cousins had all grown up. Freddie and David had emigrated to America. Valmai was married to Peter, her childhood sweetheart. Only Dyllis and Susan were still living at home. I spent many evenings in my uncle's front room with my cousin Sue. We would spend our time gossiping while listening to our favourite records. We loved Sonny and Cher's "I Got You Babe" which we played over and over again while miming to the record, taking turns to play Cher. Copying the performance that we had seen them do on Top of the Pops, we would take admiring glances at ourselves in the mirror that hung on the wall.

Lounging in my cousin's front room one Saturday afternoon, I was reminiscing about the time I had spent at Great Yarmouth when Sue casually expressed a desire to work away from home for a summer season. My heart leapt at the thought. I suggested that we could go away somewhere together. For some time we tossed the idea about, finally deciding to apply to the popular Butlin's holiday camps, where many families at that time enjoyed taking their annual summer holiday.

We wrote to the company for information. The reply told us there were numerous vacancies at the different camps scattered around the British coastline. Having little knowledge of the areas where the camps were situated, we scoured a map to discover precisely where each camp was located. Eventually we opted to work at Bognor Regis, simply because it was the furthest south.

In what seemed like no time at all, full of nervous anticipation, we were sitting in a railway carriage, travelling towards the Sussex coast. From the many different posts available, we had opted to be chalet maids. When we had completed the long process of registering at the Reception, together with the many other new recruits, we were eventually escorted to our living quarters. Sue and I listened to other fledgling chalet maids nervously laughing and chattering, whose accents came from the length and breadth of the British Isles. As we tramped through the camp, we hungrily took in everything we saw and heard as we trekked past shops, bars, restaurants and an open-air swimming pool. Above the sound of music, coming from loud speakers we observed around the camp, we could also hear the faint noise of the camp fair ground in the distance. The suitcases and bags we carried became heavier and heavier. I hoped the pretty, brightly painted two storey Swiss chalets we walked past, might be where we were to live. However, we were instructed to keep walking, because these were the campers' chalets. After passing behind the kitchens and other places the holidaymakers did not get to see, we finally reached our destination.

Reaching the farthest point of the camp from the Reception building where we had begun our journey, we were presented with the back of a row of neglected, semi-detached houses that appeared to have no relation to the camp whatsoever. The entries between the houses were boarded up, and across the top of the fences were rows of barbed wire.

We were told this was to stop people climbing over the top, ensuring only the authorised entrances to the camp were used. The fences that once separated the back gardens had been taken down to make the abandoned gardens merge into one large piece of derelict looking ground. I was horrified when we were told this sad looking sight was to be our living quarters while we worked at the camp. My heart sank, and meeting my cousin's eyes I could see she was feeling the same.

Sue and I were led to the front room of one of these shabby looking houses. Once inside, looking out of the front window I discovered the front of the house was on a quiet road going to the sea front. There were four beds in the room; a bunk bed that stood behind the door, and two single beds that partly stood in the large, square bay. Being the first to arrive, Sue and I were able to have first choice of the beds. Sue claimed the top bunk, as I threw my stuff onto one of the beds in the bay window. I was suddenly very weary from carrying my suitcases across the camp. Lying exhausted on my bed I noticed the large mural on the wall opposite the window. It showed a Spanish lady hiding her face with a fan. Surrounded by flowers, she stood in the grounds of what I supposed was a hacienda. It was a pleasant picture covering most of the wall, which made the room feel quite light and sunny.

Arriving with a second batch of Chalet maids, were two girls who came into the room, also laden with suitcases. The first girl cheerfully introduced herself as Esther. Sue and I had an instant rapport with her when she told us she was from our home town of Birmingham. Dressed in jeans, her manner seemed as casual as her dress. I was glad we were sharing the room with her. She also threw her belongings on the bed next to mine in the bay window, to claim ownership.

Our fourth roommate was very different. Rita, was from Coventry, and looked like she had come in her best clothes.

As she started to unpack, she complained there was not enough space for all her clothes that spilled out of her suitcase. I was glad Sue and I had been the first to arrive, because there wouldn't have been a draw left for our meagre belongings had Rita arrived before us. She also complained about having to take the bottom bunk. Sadly she had no choice, for no one was willing to swap with her.

Although our room was now full, there was still a lot of commotion in the house as folk continued to arrive. When the new occupants had unpacked, they spontaneously went about investigating the other rooms and introduced themselves to the rest of the household.

Sue and I also nervously joined in the exploration of the house. We discovered that Londoners were occupying the other ground floor rooms. One of their rooms also had a mural painted on one of the walls. This dark picture depicted a tiger crouching in jungle undergrowth, saliva dripping from the tiger's huge fangs. I thought it was pretty grim and was glad Sue and I had not been allocated this room.

As we investigated further, we found the upstairs residents were all from Glasgow. Although they were quite friendly, initial introductions were quite difficult because both parties had difficulty understanding each other's strong accents.

After we had unpacked and met everyone in our house, Sue and I finally went in search of the dining room. We walked into the enormous hall to see rows and rows of people sitting, eating their evening meal. All were dressed in an array of different uniforms, which was very intimidating. We imagined everyone must be aware that we were new, because we were in our civvies. Sue was so frightened she immediately turned round and walked out of the door, vowing never to return. This was as much an ordeal for me as it was for her, but I knew we had no choice but to get used to it. With some cajoling from me and a little help from her hungry stomach, we managed to persuade my cousin to go back in. As we walked into the hall again, we were arrested by a great cacophony of noise and smells. There was only a flimsy partition separating this vast canteen from the campers' dining room. Therefore with the clatter of cutlery and crockery being stacked ready to be washed, and countless people trying to converse with each other, the noise was deafening. However, by the time we had queued for our meal and found a table to sit at our panic had subsided, enabling us to freely take in the scenery around us. Looking up, Sue and I were both amused to see the array of plastic birds of every size, shape and colour imaginable hanging from the vast ceiling. After our meal we felt much more relaxed and were confident we would enjoy our time at the holiday camp.

The house was lively until the early hours of the morning. Because it was nearly everyone's first experience of living away from home, no-one was in the mood to sleep. Most of the girls assembled at the chalet office the next morning for work, were tired and bleary eyed. We were given our green and yellow overalls and shown where we could find the cleaning utensils. We were then taken to the chalet office to be given a long chain, full of master keys that would open every door on our respective chalet lines.

Entering my first chalet, I was surprised that although they looked so pretty from the outside, they were in fact, very basic. Each chalet was just a single room with a sink and a double bed, a set of cupboards and small wardrobe. Family chalets had an additional small adjoining room, housing a single or bunk bed.

Sue and I were delighted to find we were assigned to chalet lines that backed onto each other. We would often run around to each other's line to borrow cleaning materials or to help each other get finished more quickly, so that we could sit and chat. Several chalet maids would often congregate together in one of the chalets, for a long, unauthorised break.

With closed curtains, we were unobserved by any passing supervisor.

Saturdays were very hectic. The present campers departed in the morning, so all the bedclothes could be changed for the new holidaymakers arriving in the afternoon. There were teenage boys also employed to work around the chalets. It was their job to ride around on their bikes making sure none of the chalet maids ran out of essentials like sheets, pillowcases or other required commodities. I found one of them particularly attractive, so I made it my business to periodically leave my master keys inside one of the chalets. Using another set of masters one of the boys would be sent round to retrieve them. Sadly on the occasions Steve was sent to rescue my keys, he appeared totally oblivious to my existence.

Within a short time Sue and I became familiar with the routine of life at the camp, even going into the dining room failed to hold any threat for us any more. We quickly made friends from among the vast army of people that were employed there. We became so well acquainted with the young men on security, they stopped asking to see our identification passes when we passed in and out of the gates.

When Sue and I were off duty, we could usually be found in the camp's Pig and Whistle lounge bar, a favourite oasis among the staff. The venue was enormous and the bar circled the whole room, which was quite impressive when seen for the first time. All entertainment on the camp was available to the staff, except the Hawaiian Bar. However, because it was banned I desperately wanted to know what it was like inside. So having coaxed Sue to join me, we sneaked in one evening. I was glad I had seen the mock Hawaiian décor, plastic palm trees and waitress's clad in slightly scant Hawaiian costumes, for my curiosity was satisfied. However, I was rather disappointed by what I saw realising its reputation had been highly overrated.

The other place I longed to see the inside of, was the

notorious Shoreline Club. Rumours abounded among the staff of the scandalous goings on there. The club was a short distance along the sea front from the holiday camp. It stayed open from eight o'clock each Saturday evening until eight o'clock on Sunday morning. For anyone who was cool or trendy this was the place to go on a Saturday night. Strolling back to the camp late one evening, Sue and I noticed several police vans outside the Shoreline Club. Their blue lights were still whirling, casting their light on individuals standing in the crowd of onlookers, as they watched the police throw people from the club into police vans. Joining the crowd of spectators, I asked what was going on and was told it was a random drugs raid, which apparently occasionally happened. I thought it was very exciting, unlike my cousin who was horrified by what she saw and could not understand why I would want to go to such a dreadful place. Nevertheless I did, but this time Sue flatly refused to accompany me.

Another warm, balmy evening, Rita, Sue and I were enjoying a quiet drink outside a pub on the promenade. Three youths walked past that we instantly recognised. Also recognising us they backtracked, and without invitation brazenly pulled up some chairs to sit around the table with us. However we didn't mind at all because we knew them from seeing them working around the camp. One guy went to sit by Rita; he was Ronnie Crumblin from Glasgow and worked on security. The one who grabbed a chair next to Sue had worked in the kitchens and had the nickname London Johnny to differentiate him from the many other Johns and Johnnies working at the camp. The redhead who came to sit by me was none other than Steve from the chalet lines. We discovered they had all left Butlin's and were currently unemployed. The evening was filled with laughter and light-hearted banter. I could hardly believe my luck when Steve confidently took my hand when we all rose to leave. After all my inept attempts to make him notice me, I could hardly believe this was really happening. The guys escorted us back to our quarters where we arranged to meet again the following day.

Among the camp staff, the chalet maid's quarters were known as the Virgin Islands, because it was instant dismissal for any male to be found loitering around the area without permission. Nevertheless for the next couple of weeks when Rita, Sue and I were off duty, the guys would come around and sneak into our room. Esther, our fourth roommate didn't even mind when they stayed over, because she too was entertained by their clowning around. Knowing we could get into serious trouble, even instant dismissal, only added to the excitement.

However one afternoon there was a firm knock at the door, coupled with the voice of Mrs Bishop the chalet maids' manageress, asking if she could come in. Realising we were about to be caught red handed, the boys ran around the room like headless chickens, darting in different directions looking for some place to hide. Steve jumped into Esther's bed, pulling the sheets over his head. In his panic he must have imagined he couldn't be seen, even though he was sitting bolt upright. London Johnny slid underneath the bunk beds and Ronnie Crumblin jumped into Rita's bottom bunk, pulling the pillow over his head in an attempt to make it look as if he wasn't there. With bedclothes flung around the room, the place looked like it had been hit by a tornado.

The room suddenly fell deadly silent as we nervously invited Mrs Bishop to come in. She entered accompanied by the man we knew was the Head of Security. Mrs Bishop looked suitably disgusted as she surveyed the scene of chaos. Noting the cutlery, bread, jam, and margarine on top of the chest of drawers, all taken from the canteen, she reminded us of the rule that staff were not allowed to take anything out of the dinning hall. Therefore, she asked us, were we aware that we had stolen the items?

I was angry that Rita, tried hard to disassociate herself

from the situation and thought she looked utterly ridiculous as she apologised profusely, nervously wringing her hands in contrition, like Uriah Heep from the David Copperfield novel. Nevertheless, it was obvious her remonstrations fell on deaf ears, as they both ignored her.

Waiting to hear the verdict of what Mrs Bishop saw seemed like an age. In the meantime the Head of Security called the boys out from their hiding places. Only Ronnie Crumblin and Steve emerged from their refuge, Johnny stayed silently under the bunk bed. I sat rigid on the edge of mine, hoping to disguise the fact that I was shaking. I was so nervous I felt as if I could be sick.

Because I had encouraged Sue to come here I felt totally responsible for the situation we were in. I was horrified that I was on the verge of getting another of my cousins the sack. Whatever would my parents say? I looked up at my crestfallen cousin sitting on her bunk bed. Because her face was buried in her hands, it looked as if Sue was crying. However, it soon became evident she was not crying but laughing. Everyone in the room descended on her like a pack of angry animals for her insensitivity to this grave situation. She quickly apologised saying it was all the tension in the room that made her giggle. She later confessed to me, it was because she knew John was still hiding under her bed that had really made her laugh.

Because Mrs Bishop and the Head of Security only found Ronnie and Steve in the room, they gave us the benefit of the doubt that no licentious behaviour had taken place. However, we received a humiliating dressing down in front of the boys for behaving like shameless harlots, stealing and not keeping our room clean. When they left they took Steve and Ronnie with them.

Johnny eventually came out from under the bunk bed when we were sure they would not return. We all burst out laughing when we saw him, because he was covered in thick fluff that had accumulated under the bed. His jet black hair was now pale grey. Because all the windows had been nailed shut, we weren't sure how to get Johnny out of the room and off the premises; therefore we were greatly relieved when we saw Steve and Ronnie wandering up the road toward the house a short time later. We hoped they might by able to help get him out. On closer inspection, we discovered some nails were a bit loose on one of the little windows at the top of the bay. With the aid of one of the kitchen knives we had taken from the dining room, the three boys managed to prise the window open. It was fortunate that Johnny was slim because the window was so small. With a lot of pushing and shoving, grunting and a lot of giggling, like a baby being born he eventually slithered through the window, landing with a thud onto the ground outside. Fortunately only his dignity was injured from the experience. Now that the whole episode was over, out of sheer relief we all laughed until tears ran down our faces, as we talked about what had happened. When we finally calmed down, we girls were disappointed when we heard from inside our room, the boys discuss going back home. As we watched them disappear down the road we didn't realise this would be the last time we would ever see them.

Butlin's seemed a very empty place when it became evident the three boys had really gone for good. However, because of this sad episode, an unexpected friendship was born with one of the Scottish girls from upstairs in the house. Her name was Anne Mackie. She had met Steve at the infamous Shoreline club and they had become good friends. Now that he was gone, Anne and I reminisced about him continually, because she missed him too. I had resented her friendship with Steve, although during these chats I discovered that I liked her very much, and realised why Steve had wanted to be her friend.

Anne liked to think she was a hippy. It made me laugh to

see her handing out wild flowers to visitors at the entrance gate to Butlin's, telling them things like 'Peace' and 'Love' as they walked in. When she invited me to go along to the Shoreline club with her, our friendship was sealed.

The Shoreline was every bit as exciting as I had imagined. Although it wasn't as large as I thought it would be, everything about it seemed to assault my senses. I had never before seen the strange, dim, bluish lighting that caused pale colours to look startlingly white, which I later discovered was ultraviolet lighting. The dark labyrinth of passages led to intimate corners, where comfy chairs and couches provided a place for people to lounge or sleep as the night wore on. It was the first time I had heard the music of the likes of Otis Redding, Sam and Dave, Aretha Franklin and other Motown artists, which I immediately fell in love with. I hardly sat down all night; it was difficult not to dance to such great music.

A dance competition took place each week, although not many people entered because the regular three black male competitors and the large white girl, who was surprisingly light on her feet, could dance everyone else off the floor. Anyway, it was far more entertaining to watch them, than to attempt to compete against them.

At daybreak, I sat with other flagging revellers in the Shoreline's cafe, to sleepily watch the waves crashing onto the shore, before heading for home. I had not been disappointed at all, this time, by what I found inside these premises.

A week or two later, in my absence, a discussion developed in the house were I lived, between Sue and some of the Scottish girls from upstairs. They had become dissatisfied with working at the camp and wanted to try their luck at finding work in one of the restaurants or coffee shops in the town; of which many had situation vacant signs in their windows. Apparently as more people joined the conversation the decision to leave became infectious. The small circle of girls, who had originally thought about leaving, had grown into a crowd. A short time later while I was busily working on my chalets, my cousin, accompanied by what appeared to be all the Scottish girls from our house, came walking up my line. Among them was my friend Anne Mackie. Sue said abruptly "We have all decided to leave." I was taken aback by this news, because Sue and I had never discussed leaving Butlin's. Nevertheless, I felt I could not let my cousin go without me, so I agreed to join them.

After I had put my cleaning materials away, I went with this laughing throng of chalet maids to the camp chalet office. Having previously been humiliated by Mrs Bishop, I was vengefully looking forward to seeing the look on her face, when told this small army were not only resigning, but were about to walk off the camp that very day. However, she did not seem at all fazed by the news, explaining that a considerable amount of paper work needed to be completed. Therefore it would not be until late afternoon that we would eventually be able to leave. So we would have very little chance of getting accommodation that night. She advised us to re-consider and leave the following day in order to give the office staff adequate time to process the necessary paper work. She wisely knew that by the next day the current mood would probably have evaporated, and we would change our minds about leaving. Like ducks on a shooting range she demolished every argument voiced in opposition to her suggestion, until nearly everyone's resolve had ebbed away. Even my cousin succumbed to her clever wheedling and agreed to stay on. From the dozen or more girls who were so adamant about resigning that Sunday morning, Mrs Bishop had managed to whittle the number down to two determined chalet maids, who refused to be manipulated by her velvet tongue.

Chapter 7

Pompey

At four o'clock that afternoon, outside the gate with our suitcases, a week's wages in our pocket but nowhere to go stood Anne Mackie and me. However, not knowing where I would sleep that night didn't worry me at all. I found it rather exciting; in fact it was all part of the adventure that I hoped, lay ahead.

From a telephone box near the camp, Anne phoned a fellow Glaswegian she knew from the Shoreline club, for advice. He was currently living along the coast in Portsmouth. Jock, as he was called, was known to nearly everyone who went to the Shoreline, because he was the main drug dealer. He suggested we go and stay with him until we decided what we were going to do, which is exactly what Anne hoped he would say. So with the directions to his flat in our heads, we dragged our luggage onto the next bus heading for Portsmouth.

After a long and exhausting journey we reached his flat at about eight in the evening. I don't know what I was expecting to see when we rang his doorbell, but I was very nervous, because I had not previously met this man, whose reputation I knew well. However, when he opened the door to us I was surprised at how ordinary he looked. Casually dressed in jeans and tee shirt, he seemed very friendly. As he led us up to his flat, my apprehensions about meeting him melted away.

We were generously allowed to use Jock's bed that first night. However, during the following weeks of our stay Anne and I were relegated to sleeping on the floor. We didn't mind though, because there was moderately more room on the floor than being crammed together into that little bed.

To describe Jock's lodgings as a flat was a gross over

statement. It was just a small, furnished attic. There was a small kitchen table and two chairs nestling under the eave, to the right of the door. The bed was along the opposite wall and facing the door was a sideboard. The old-fashioned furniture seemed to swamp the limited space. A small Belling cooker sat on the sideboard, but Jock told us he didn't use it much, because there was a cheap café just around the corner.

The facilities at the flat were practically non-existent; we did most of our washing in the bathroom downstairs. Utensils and our smalls were washed in a bowl placed on the little kitchen table, which meant we were continually running up and down the stairs with bowls of water, spilling everywhere. We disposed of the dirty water by throwing it out of the little window. I was surprised that no one complained. I was also surprised that nothing was said about our laundry being dried by laying it out across the hot tiled roof under the jutting window.

Jock hardly ever turned anyone down who asked for board for the night. While Anne and I were there, three more guys asked for refuge for a night or two. So for several nights there were five of us sleeping like sardines on the limited floor- space.

The first Saturday we had spent at Jock's flat, as a gift, he gave Anne and me some free 'amph' (Amphetamine), before we went to the Shoreline club to enhance the experience. The following weeks we were expected to pay for it. I was rather apprehensive about taking it for the first time, but as both Jock and Anne had no such qualms, not wanting to look naïve, I also took it.

The effects of the 'amph' began to kick in by the time we arrived at the club. I was relieved to find the feelings were no different from those I experienced when I took the black capsules prescribed by my doctor, back home. These had been given to me to suppress my appetite and to aid weight loss. They were known on the black market as Black Bombers.

I told no one at the time, but I celebrated my nineteenth birthday at the beloved Shoreline club. As a child, I had been disappointed too many times, when the day failed to live up to my childish expectations, so I had ceased to acknowledge the occasion. Nevertheless, I took great delight in being at the hallowed Shoreline club on my birthday, and felt like I was enjoying my own private party.

Within weeks, Anne and I had found our own flat. However, we were really sad to leave Jock's pad. Even though the flat had been quite primitive, and sometimes overcrowded we had enjoyed being there so much. Not only because Jock had been very kind to us, but also it had been such fun to meet the many different people that we had seen pass through his flat. I loved this new life style I had been introduced to.

The flat Anne and I rented together was a spacious, ground floor bed-sitter. It was down one of the roads leading to the sea front at Southsea, near Portsmouth, and close to Jock's flat. It housed all the necessary basic amenities, and also had a large comfy settee, cosily sitting in the middle of the room in front of the large fireplace. It also had the luxury of a sink. We could do any washing in the flat we needed, without having to wade through the house with bowls of water spilling everywhere. There was also a little Belling cooker, rarely used for anything other than toast. Compared to living at Jock's place, this flat was a mansion, and to sleep in a bed again after weeks on the floor, was bliss. Sometimes Anne and I would buy hamburgers from the Wimpy bar, on the promenade near our flat. Compared to what we had recently been used to, it felt like sheer luxury to be able chat across the room to each other late into the night, while snuggled up in our beds, eating our burgers with a cup of hot tea.

Even though it was a great distance to travel, Anne and I continued to attend the Shoreline club. Most Sunday mornings, along with other local clubbers, we would get a lift home from a van owning neighbour, who also frequented the club. Before heading home, we would join the horde of tired people who, like a shoal of fish, would wend their way to the café along the sea front, for a last cup of tea or coffee. This was to delay departure until the last possible minute, in an attempt to ring the last dregs out of the Saturday night experience.

At the other end of our journey the passengers would spill out of the overcrowded vehicle and into our flat, where Anne and I happily served tea and buttered toast to our guests. Not until early afternoon did most people feel ready to wander home.

Although the club was also open on Wednesday evenings, it wasn't nearly as well attended as it was on Saturday evenings because it was too far for many to travel midweek. One rare occasion Anne and I decided to go along but on leaving we discovered we had missed the last train back to Portsmouth. My cousin Sue was still working at Butlin's, and through her I knew there were now two vacant beds in my old room. Anne and I walked along the sea front hoping we might be able to sleep the night there.

Looking through the window, I was relieved to see Sue sitting on her bed. She told us we were welcome to stay, if we were able to get past the Security guards. Anne and I went round the corner to the camp entrance, and brazenly walked through the gate, straight into the camp past the Security guard. He obviously thought we still worked there because he called out "Hi" to us as we passed him. We hoped we could walk out of the camp as easily as we came in.

Getting out of the camp the next morning proved to be much more difficult than it had been to get in. We walked to the same gate that we had entered the previous evening, only to find the Security guard on duty was a new recruit, so he didn't recognise us. Not having identification passes to show him, we turned round and went back into the house. We needed to work out how we were to escape. Going upstairs to the bathroom, I noticed through the open window the bathroom was near the front of the house, past the barbed wire fencing. I called Anne to come up and take a look, suggesting we could climb out of the window and jump off the drainpipe to freedom. Anne was not convinced this was a good idea. So, to prove my point, I got out of the window with the intention of jumping first. However, standing on the drainpipe outside the bathroom window, I realised it was much higher than it had appeared from inside, and it wasn't such a good idea to jump after all.

With Anne's help I tried to clamber back into the bathroom. However, I caught my favourite blue, needle cord dress, on the little rod sticking up from the window frame. Every time Anne attempted to pull me back into the bathroom, I could hear my dress tearing. The more I struggled to get in through the window, the higher my dress was creeping up my body, exposing more and more of my stocking tops and flesh to the passing traffic on the pavement below. It didn't help, that I started giggling at the absurdity of the situation. I could not believe that no pedestrian on the street below appeared to be at all daunted by the sight of a pair of legs waving from the bathroom window. When Anne finally managed to haul me back into the bathroom, we sat on the floor laughing until we ached.

However, we still had the problem of how to get off the camp. Eventually after much debate, we decided to walk round to the gate at the farthest point from the chalet maid's quarters. Only a small number of holidaymakers and hardly any staff ever used this entrance, because of its remote location. We were very nervous as we approached, wondering what we would do if we were asked to show our passes. Nevertheless we walked through the gate, relieved that the Security guard didn't even look up from the newspaper he was reading. We were free!

Anne and I lived in Portsmouth for several more months, and saw life settle into a much more mundane routine. Working in a local box-making factory was boring, as living in our little flat was becoming. It was the end of the season, and seeing our friends, one by one, migrate back to their places of origin, made us realise it was time for us to do the same.

A few weeks later Anne and I stood on the platform at Victoria coach station in London, waiting for our coaches to take us home. We exchanged phone numbers and said we would definitely meet in the future, although we couldn't possibly see how it could happen, living so far apart. As I watched Anne board the coach that was taking her to Glasgow, it was with a great sense of sadness that I waved goodbye.

I was very pensive during my journey back to Birmingham, I did not want to go back to my humdrum life again after experiencing the liberty and adventure of that magical summer of 1967.

Chapter 8

I'll take the High Road

As the coach finally swung into the familiar Digbeth coach station in Birmingham, I saw my parents waiting. I was grateful to my father for volunteering to drive me home; since my luggage seemed to have greatly increased in weight during the months I had been away.

Once I was settled at home, my primary task was to catch up with old friends. It was great to see Lorraine again, and I was delighted when she invited me to visit her grandmother again. I desperately wanted to know what the future held, so I was anxious to have my cards read.

When later, Lorraine and I were drinking tea in her grandmother's living room, I giggled with delight when Mrs Hughes finally laid the cards across the coffee table. As she began to read them, she told me I would be leaving Birmingham within the number three: three days, three weeks or three months. "Oh not again, she's only just arrived home!" giggled Lorraine. I laughed too, and told Mrs Hughes the cards were wrong. I had no intention of leaving Birmingham so soon.

I also enjoyed rekindling the friendship of a previous colleague, Mary Carter, with whom I had become good friends when employed for a short time at the same firm. While we had eaten our sandwiches during the lunch break, we had swapped stories about our home lives. I found Mary's account of her childhood spent in a Children's home, both fascinating and harrowing. Hearing about my somewhat turbulent life at home, she had kindly invited me to stay with her and her husband, whom she had only recently married, if conditions became too difficult. Although grateful for her generosity, I assured her I didn't think it would ever become necessary.

Sitting at home watching television with my family on Saturday evenings was agony. I would look at the clock on the mantelpiece, and think about the people who were probably dancing the night away at the Shoreline Club, at that very moment, as I had done until recently. I never imagined it was possible to miss anything as much as I missed living on the Sussex coast.

I loved to receive letters with a Glasgow postmark, knowing they were from my hippy friend Anne. Just to see the brightly decorated letters fall on the hall carpet made me smile. There were so many flowers and slogans, such as MAKE LOVE NOT WAR and FLOWER POWER written on the envelope, there was hardly any room for the address.

Anne and I telephoned each other every Sunday afternoon. I would wait in eager anticipation for the telephone to ring in the red telephone box, just around the corner from my home. After a brief conversation I would then return the call, in order to share the cost. It was comforting to know Anne pined for Portsmouth as much as I did.

Because of the tension at home, the eruption I had anticipated, finally happened one evening when my mother left the house to do her cleaning job at the Kalamazoo. My father was also getting ready to go to work on the night shift. He warned me to ignore my ten-year-old brother if he misbehaved while he was out of the house, informing me he would punish my brother when he returned home the next morning, if necessary. However, Bryn gleefully took note of our conversation, knowing any mischief he got up to during the evening, would be forgotten by the next day.

When our father disappeared out of the back door, believing he had gone to work, Bryn immediately began his offensive to annoy me. My brother knew how much I loved Top of the Pops that I was watching on the television that night, so he made as much noise as possible to make it difficult for me to hear. When I failed to be provoked, his second attempt was to stand in front of the television waving his arms so that I couldn't see the screen. Unexpectedly our father returned, having only gone to the outside lavatory before setting off for work. Realising he had been caught red-handed, Bryn instantly jumped into our father's armchair and looked up at him with wide-eyed innocence, as I acquainted our father with Bryn's timely display of mischievous behaviour.

Like a spark to dry tinder my father's temper was immediately ignited. To protect himself from the blows, Bryn curled himself up into a ball as our father repeatedly hit him. As if waking from a trance, my father realised what he was doing. His face was contorted with rage as he turned on me. With clenched fists he moved towards me, but stopped dead in his tracks before he struck a blow. I was trembling with fear as he said in a low voice, "That's it you bastard, I want you out of this house!" As he began to put his coat on against the cold night air, he apologised to Bryn for what he had done. He told me he had never hit Bryn before and it was my fault that he had done it now. "No one really wants you here." He told me. "We all dread it when it's time for you to come back home". He snarled, "I mean it. You had better get somewhere else to live, because I want you out of this house by next week!" As soon as he left the house my fourteen-year-old sister Gail, who had been sitting in silence while this furore ensued, ran to sit with my brother. This was partly to comfort him, partly to show where her loyalty lay.

When the clock on the wall later told us it was time for our mother to leave work, Gail and Bryn put on their coats and left the house. I knew from past experience it was their intention to stand outside the factory gate until she appeared. This was so they would be the first to tell our mother their side of the evening's events, in order to get her on their side. I knew their plan had worked when I was ignored as my mother walked into the house via the back door.

Feeling totally dejected, I decided it might be better for everyone if I did just go away. My legs felt heavy as I slowly climbed the stairs to my bedroom. I wrote a letter to Mary Carter, asking if I could possibly take up her offer of accommodation, until I could find somewhere more permanent to live. I posted the letter immediately, so that I could not change my mind. There was no going back now.

Answering the front door a few days later, I hardly recognised Mary's husband Ken, who was dressed from head to toe in his black leather motorbike gear. Taking off his helmet, he told me that Mary had received my letter and they were both happy for me to live with them. He had come to collect as many of my belongings as we could carry on the back of his motorbike, before the day I would eventually move in.

When we got back to their house, I told her I would not impose upon her and Ken's good nature for any longer than I had to. When I attempted to tell her how indebted I felt for their generous hospitality, Mary just laughed and told me I could stay with them for as long as I liked. Nevertheless I resolved to get a bed-sitter or flat to be out of their way as soon as I could.

The Saturday that I had arranged to move to Mary's house, I awoke early to find the grey, dismal day matched my sombre mood perfectly. I had hoped that a member of my family might be compelled to speak to me, not knowing when they may see me again. I was wrong! I went downstairs to face the same wall of silence I had endured all week.

I listened to the radio for a few hours; waiting for what I thought was a reasonable time to deposit myself at my friend's house. Just as I was about to leave, there was the sound of footsteps coming down the side entry of our house. I waited expectantly, wondering who our visitors could be. It turned out to be my cousin Valmai and her husband Peter, who very rarely visited us. My surprised parents profusely welcomed them as they stepped into the sun lounge at the back of our house. I felt that I had no choice but to stay and join the superficial conversation. Over a cup of tea, I realised Val had come for some information about her sister Susan, knowing I heard from her more than anyone else in the family. To the embarrassment of my parents, Valmai asked if I was glad to be home again. I answered with fake joviality that I was, not willing to expose the current situation. Finally, when I felt I couldn't stand the pretence any longer, I said blithely, "Oh well, I must go".

My father followed me from the sun lounge, as I walked through the kitchen to go out of the house through the front door. When he knew we were out of hearing range of the visiting relatives, he quietly told me I could stay if I wanted to. It was an awkward moment for both of us when I declined his offer. I felt it was too late to reconsider, now that all my possessions were at Mary's house. As I closed the front door behind me I thought my heart would break. I wondered when or if I would ever see my family again.

I was standing alone at the bus stop when it began to rain in earnest. Raindrops mingled with my tears that were now running freely down my face. I felt there was a great lonely, aching hole inside and I didn't know how to fill it.

When I arrived at Mary's house, she escorted me to the bedroom she had prepared. I wanted to cry all over again when I saw the great effort she had made to make it comfortable for me.

That first Sunday at Mary's house, I phoned Anne Mackie as usual from a nearby telephone box. During the conversation I was told Anne's mother also wanted to talk to me. Never having had any previous contact with her, I was intrigued to know what it was about, and shocked when I heard Anne's mother invite me to go and live in Glasgow with their family. Naturally, I immediately rejected the offer, but she was very insistent, giving me a catalogue of reasons why I should go. First I hadn't a job yet, so I could look for employment in Glasgow instead of Birmingham. Then she carried on to say no matter how welcoming Mary and Ken were to me, newly weds need to be alone, also demolishing every argument of why I should not go. Mrs Mackie told me the whole family was in agreement with her proposal. This generous stranger even wanted to send me the money for the coach fare, should I agree. When Anne came back onto the phone she continued to coax me, describing the places we could go together and the fun we would have. The more she talked, the more I was persuaded it might be a good idea.

Later that evening I sheepishly discussed with Mary the possibility of going to live in Scotland. She had so lovingly prepared the spare bedroom that leaving my new home so soon made me feel I was betraying our friendship. However, she waived away my apologies and encouraged me to go to Scotland, telling me what an exciting opportunity she thought it was for me. Our conversation finally sealed my decision.

Within a few days I was again standing at Digbeth coach station, this time waiting for the coach that would take me to Glasgow. True to Mrs Hughes prediction it was less than three weeks since I was last here, having just arrived back home from my adventure in Portsmouth. It seemed incredible that I was leaving Birmingham again so soon.

Settled in my seat on the coach, I couldn't understand why the passengers were each handed a blanket. However, as we continued to travel through the evening and into the night, I appreciated how valuable the blankets were in helping to keep us warm, as we tried to sleep during the long journey. As dawn began to break I became more and more nervous, and wondered if I had been wise to come here. However, when I spied Anne through the coach window as it pulled into the Glasgow bus station, my fears lifted.

I wearily took my first glimpse of Glasgow through the dirty windows of the corporation bus taking us to the district of Cadder, where Anne lived. I was surprised to see how grey and shabby some of the buildings looked. When I commented about them to Anne, I was told these buildings were called tenements. This place seemed very different from my own home town.

When we arrived at our journey's end, I was horrified when Anne pointed out her 'house' to me, for it was a flat, on the ground floor of a three-storey block and I was about to discover it also only had two bedrooms. Although we had discussed our homes in Portsmouth, I had wrongly believed Anne lived in a three bed roomed semi-detached house as I did. Knowing there were already five people living there I was rather concerned about what they were going to do with me.

I nervously walked down the concrete steps towards Anne's home, apprehensive at the prospect of meeting her family. However, I needn't have worried, as I followed Anne in through the front door, without waiting to be introduced Mrs Mackie gave me a big hug as if she had always known me. I was surprised at how different she was from her daughter Anne, who was very slender and had rather sharp features. By contrast everything about Anne's mum was round. Her kind eyes twinkled so much they seemed to light up her face, which was so shiny it looked as if it had been polished.

Walking into the living room I found Anne's two younger sisters standing to attention, obviously as nervous as I was. Anne introduced the giggling children as wee Margaret and wee Carol. Wee Margaret who was twelve was skinny like Anne, and was the only member of the family who had dark hair. Wee Carol, who closely resembled her mother, was seven and sported the same basin hairstyle of her older sister.

Apparently, everyone in Glasgow was called wee or big depending on their size. Everyone became a little more relaxed when Mrs Mackie eventually entered the room carrying a tray full of sandwiches and cakes, to be eaten with the tea she had promised. I was to learn it was a Glaswegian custom that a cup of tea was rarely given without an accompanying feast.

Anne helped me take my suitcases into the larger of the two small bedrooms, which I was told I would be sharing with her. However, I was embarrassed to find it was her parents' bedroom and they were moving out for the duration of my stay, to sleep on the bed settee in the living room. Mrs Mackie told me she didn't mind this arrangement at all and neither did her husband. Anne's two younger sisters continued to sleep in the smaller bedroom they had previously shared with Anne.

Later Mrs Gorman, Mrs Mackie's middle-aged friend, who lived in the flat on the other side of the hallway or 'close' as it was called here, came to have a look at the wee English lassie. She looked quite impoverished, her dark, greying, greasy hair hung limply on her thin, hunched shoulders. Through the thick lenses of her glasses, I could see that her eyes seemed to work independent of each other. I was so tired that I had trouble deciding which eye to focus on. She seemed friendly enough though. Trying to hold a conversation with her was quite tiring because of the difficulty I had understanding her very pronounced accent. I later found Glaswegians had the same trouble understanding my broad Birmingham accent!

After so much activity during the day, I was glad when bedtime came. Anne had put an old poster on her mum's bedroom wall advertising the Shoreline Club, to make the surroundings seem a little more familiar for me. Seeing it brought memories flooding back of the preceding months we had spent together on the South coast. We lay in bed that night reminiscing about our experiences in Bognor Regis and Portsmouth. Talking about some of the people we had known made me feel quite nostalgic. The anxiety I had felt over the recent days about coming here melted away as I drifted off to sleep.

While Anne was at work the next day, Mrs Mackie took me into Glasgow, where she bought me a new winter coat to protect against the often harsh, Glaswegian winter. I was bewildered by such generosity from someone I hardly knew, especially as I now realised the family weren't very well off.

I had thought I would look for employment in an office when I came to Glasgow, however Anne worked on the buses and asked me to join her. I could see she loved the work, she told me the wages were very good too. It appeared the population of Glasgow were divided between those on the dole and those who worked on transport, for it soon became evident that jobs here were few and far between. I didn't want to remain unemployed and be a burden to Mrs Mackie, therefore I decided to apply for a job on the Central SMT (Scottish Motor Transport), feeling delighted that I might possibly be working with my friend Anne.

I was at home with Mrs Mackie one afternoon, waiting for my application to be processed by the bus company, when there was a knock at the door. I felt rather timid when I realised the caller was the infamous Rob Carruthers I had heard so much about. He lived a few closes down the road with his parents, who were friends of the Mackies. His reputation had travelled all the way down to Bognor Regis, where I had heard many unsavoury stories about him from Glaswegians who worked there. He was the leader of a gang called the Fleet. I understood he had spent most of his twenty odd years in remand homes and prisons, mainly for crimes of violence through gang warfare. I heard him tell Mrs Mackie he had brought some of his favourite Long Playing records round for the 'wee English lassie' to listen to, concerned that I didn't get too bored while Anne was out at work all day. I was astonished by this amazingly thoughtful gesture from a complete stranger who had not even set eyes on me yet.

I had heard a lot about the Glasgow gangs from Anne and also from Ronnie Crumblin in Bognor, who had been a member of a gang called the Tongs before going to work at Butlin's. Gang warfare was commonplace here. I had been so incredulous when I first saw a youth with a slash mark across his face that Anne had delighted in telling me gory stories of fights she had witnessed. When a fight broke out in a club where she was enjoying a night out with her girl friends, a guy she knew was badly slashed with a razor blade. Anne told me it had fallen to her to hold the gaping bloody wound together until they managed to get him to the hospital.

The local gossip was still rife about the murder of The Mad Spaniard, as people called him, who had gone to England to get away from the gangs, a couple of years before I came. When he came home to visit family he was stabbed to death by a rival gang member.

I had not envisaged just how different Glasgow would be from my native city of Birmingham. I was beginning to realise that I had not only come to a different city but a different country.

Before I left Birmingham, I sent my mother a letter informing her that I was going to live in Glasgow. It was not long after my arrival that Carol quietly knocked on the door of the bedroom I was sharing with Anne. Seeing I was awake, she handed me a letter that had arrived from home. Recognising my mother's handwriting on the envelope I hastily opened it. I read that my parents were heartbroken because I had not visited them before I left. Nevertheless, the door was always open for me, if I wished to return. A second letter dropped from the envelope onto the bed. I saw from the handwriting it was from my mischievous little brother Bryn. He begged me to come home, telling me that my mum cried all the time because she missed me so much. Burying my face in the pillow so that no one could hear me, I sobbed bitterly, suddenly feeling very homesick.

Chapter 9

On the buses

In hardly any time at all the wait was over, and it was time to commence the required two weeks training course, which took place in the classroom at the bus depot at Old Kilpatrick, Renfewshire. I began with several other new recruits, who would also eventually work at the depot. We were taught to use a ticket machine and to balance the figures on a form called a waybill, which had to be completed at the end of every shift. We also had to memorise all the fare stages on every bus route that ran from the station. We learned to recite the bus stages parrot fashion, ready to be tested on them in front of the class at the end of the course. Having this knowledge was of great value to the cadets who were familiar with the area. However, being able to recite the fare stages wasn't very advantageous to a complete stranger, because I had no idea where they were anyway.

Something I had not been taught at the training school, but soon learned from the more experienced conductors once out on the road, was the art of pilfering money from the bus company. It was common practice by the crews and passengers alike, to conspire together to keep as much money from the bus company as possible. The conductor would brazenly ask likely passengers if they wanted a ticket. If the answer was no, the passenger would receive back part of the fare, with the conductor pocketing the rest. So common was the practice, many passengers would even tell the conductor to keep the ticket in order to get a reduced fare.

The bus routes from Old Kilpatrick depot were mainly around the surrounding districts of Clydebank. Many of the passengers were employed at the giant Clyde shipbuilders, and Singer the sewing machine company. When it was clocking off time at either of these factories, Clydebank would swarm with workers eager to return home after a hard day's grind. Buses would already be lined up behind one another outside the factories, waiting to take this great army of people to their destinations. Sometimes the buses would be so overcrowded, the conductor could not pass down the aisle to collect the fares. They would stand in the road happily receiving the passengers' fares while the factory workers alighted from the bus, often not even venturing to offer a ticket.

From the Old Kilpatrick depot the buses also travelled to beauty spots like the village of Helensburgh and to the outskirts of Loch Lomond. Therefore I had the opportunity to see some of the stunning Scottish countryside.

It was an unwritten rule among the bus crews that the conductor always paid for the driver's meal when they took a break at the designated Transport cafés. This was the driver's reward for watching out for inspectors on the road and warning the conductor if they saw one lurking ahead, for fiddling money from the bus company was a hazardous business. The inspectors were not ignorant of the illegal practices because most of them had been promoted from among the ranks themselves. Daily guerrilla warfare existed between the bus crews and the inspectors, zealous to catch employees at their illicit practices. The penalty was instant dismissal if a passenger was found travelling without a ticket. It had even been known for conductors to be prosecuted, but that was rare.

Walking into the staff canteen for the first time I was shocked to see the words f*** McGovern daubed across one of the walls in giant letters. However, it was not long before I understood why there was so much contempt felt for this particularly devious inspector, who would use some bizarre methods to discover which crews were involved in this fraudulent exercise. Aware that the bus drivers would be on the look out, he would hide in public lavatories or behind bushes and trees to avoid being seen until the last possible minute, giving little or no time for the driver to warn the conductor.

Arguments between male colleagues always had the potential to spill over into a brawl. Arriving back at the depot late one evening at the end of a shift, a great deal of commotion could be heard coming from the canteen. It was obvious there was a fight going on inside. As my bus pulled into the depot, so did two police cars. The occupants of the police car hastily jumped out and ran towards the noise. Other bus crews were already standing around outside, waiting to see what would happen next. One of the middle-aged conductors quietly asked me if I would look after something for him while the police were around. When I agreed, he led me round to the rear of a bus, where he pulled, from inside his coat, a giant knife. My failure to be surprised that he carried this weapon made me realise how integrated I was becoming into the culture of this extraordinary place.

Drivers and conductors would often wave in acknowledgment as they passed one another on the road. On the whole there was a great deal of loyalty and camaraderie between colleagues, especially between a driver and his conductor. If a crew were particularly busy, some drivers would unofficially change the name of the destination on the front of the bus to one not required by the waiting passengers, to avoid picking them up. When the bus had passed the waiting queue the driver would then revert to the correct destination plate.

Anne and I enjoyed an active social life, most weekends when we were off duty, we could be found dancing with Anne's friends at the 'Barrowland' or 'Lacano', popular venues in Glasgow's city centre. There was much social activity after a hard day at work. We would join colleagues at a local pub, to wind down before returning home, and parties held by colleagues were commonplace. However, my greatest pleasure by far was just sitting in the staff canteen having a 'carry on and blather' with the other young bus conductors before the afternoon shift began. Like Anne I loved being a clippie.

One evening during a late shift my foot began to throb, the pain steadily increased as the night wore on. I had noticed a small cut on one of my toes earlier in the day, so during a quiet period I decided to inspect it. I discovered the toe had become quite infected. It was swollen and bright yellow.

Unfortunately, I failed to take my ticket machine off before taking a look at my toe. To my horror, as I lifted my foot onto an unoccupied seat, I dislodged the heavy machine from its holder. It hit my throbbing toe before crashing onto the floor of the bus. My foot had become so swollen that once I had taken off my shoe I couldn't get it back on again. By the end of the shift, the pain was so bad, I felt sure I must have broken a bone when the ticket machine landed on my foot.

Returning to the depot, my supervisor told me to go immediately to the Casualty Department of the local hospital and so I was taken tearfully to the Glasgow Royal Infirmary by one of the drivers. After several hours at the hospital, an x-ray revealed I had no broken bones, although my foot had been severely bruised by the accident. Nevertheless, back at home, the excruciating pain kept me awake for most of the night.

As instructed by the doctor in the hospital, I went to see my GP the following morning. He gave me antibiotics and a sick note to take a couple of weeks off work to recuperate. To my shock while examining my foot, without telling me what he was about to do, the GP swiftly lanced my toe and squeezed the poison out of my offending digit. I let out such a piecing scream it could be heard by terrified waiting patients and half way down the street!

Having given my waybill, ticket machine and moneybag to colleagues who had volunteered to balance my evening's takings for me, I wondered how much money would be left after they had taken their cut from this unexpected windfall. I was concerned, because whatever amount of money was deficient I knew I would personally have to make up. However returning to work, I discovered the fear of having my money stolen by my colleagues had been unfounded. Not only had my fellow conductors handed in the correct amount of money to the cashier, but they had also saved the money I had 'fiddled', until I was well enough to return to work and collect it. I felt quite ashamed at how badly I had misjudged my colleagues, and wondered if I would ever understand these inscrutable people.

Although I encountered a minor amount of prejudice because I was English, most people I met were incredibly kind to me. One very cold winter's day I was conducting a bus on the small Clydebank to Drumchapel circuit. A woman stood for ages at one of the bus stops, shivering with the cold, waiting for my bus to return. She had earlier been a passenger and thought I looked so cold that she bought me a pair of knee length socks from a local shop, and waited for my bus, in order to give them to me.

Several times on the cold, dark winter evenings, I saw the same group of twelve-year-old boys waiting for my bus. They managed to persuade me to hand money over to them, by telling me they wanted to buy fish suppers for my driver and me to eat during our supper break at the terminus. I felt foolish the first time I gave them money. Seeing them jubilantly jump off my bus I was quite sure I would never see either them or my money again. However, when I later saw these exuberant youngsters waiting at the bus stop with the fish suppers, I realised I had misjudged them. Each time I gave them money they would always dutifully wait for us at the pre-arranged bus stop in Clydebank, with my fish suppers in hand.

Payment for their kind deeds was a free ride to the Drumchapel terminus, where they would stay on the bus during our break and attempt to teach me Irish rebel songs. One of the boys would accompany the singing on his harmonica, which apparently he carried everywhere he went. Both my driver and I were always greatly entertained by the impromptu performance.

It was common practice for young, confident conductors to casually jump off the open backed buses, before they had completely stopped. I also absent-mindedly did the same when, to my horror I realised the vehicle was going faster than I had imagined. Having just finished the shift, my bus was entering the depot when my feet failed to keep up with the speed of the bus and I fell flat on my face, grazing my hands and knees. My tears were of humiliation rather than pain, when I saw my colleagues standing in the middle of the road to stop the traffic, so they could collect the coins that were scattered over the busy road. I was mortified because it happened at the busiest time of day, when most of the crews were either drifting back into the garage after the early shift, or were coming in to prepare for the afternoon shift.

To help salvage some of my bruised dignity, over a medicinal cup of tea in the canteen, my colleagues told me I was now a fully-fledged conductor. For I was not the first to have the embarrassing experience of falling off a bus; most drivers and conductors had taken a tumble at one time or another. To help laugh away my tears everyone had a story to tell of other accidents that had happened at the depot. The most amusing was of the driver who caught his trouser leg on the hand brake, as he was about to jump down from his cabin. Not only was he stopped in his tracks, he was suspended upside down until one of his colleagues managed to stop laughing long enough to free him.

The company provided a staff bus to take employees, who

had no transport of their own (which was nearly everyone) back to Glasgow at the end of the night, because public buses had stopped running. The bus would stop at intermittent points in the city, so that staff could catch the Corporation night service to complete their journey home. It was often fun on these journeys, relieved their working day was over the mood was usually buoyant. Good-humoured horseplay would even occasionally erupt between the youthful young men. At each of the stops in the city the last person to leave the bus was supposed to ring the bell, to indicate to the driver it was safe to move off again. However, it was common for someone to press the bell before everyone was off the bus, leaving the last couple of people having to jump from the moving vehicle as it gathered momentum again.

Unfortunately, one particular night I happened to be the last remaining person standing on the platform. Not wanting to lose face or be left behind I bravely jumped off the bus, even though I wasn't at all sure I would land safely. As soon as my feet touched the ground my knees buckled under me. I landed on my back and bounced several feet down the road before coming to a halt. I heard the bus screech to a halt as anxious voices raced toward me. I was embarrassed beyond belief that I had so soon fallen off another bus. I wished the ground would open up and swallow me, but it didn't. Therefore, although I wasn't injured I lay motionless on the ground, with my eyes closed. When I felt people gently nudging me to see if I was conscious, I dutifully groaned a little and opened my eyes to see what looked like a thousand pair of eyes peering down at me. Helped by concerned colleagues, with my ripped stockings hanging by a thread, I slowly stood to my feet and walked a little to prove to everyone I was all right. Minutes later when everyone was satisfied I was not damaged in any way, the crowd dispersed as individuals continued their journey home, as did I while vowing I would never fall off a bus again.

Whilst living in Scotland, I found it baffling to find how much hostility was generated by religion. I didn't understand why Catholics and Protestants didn't seem to like each other very much. No-one I knew from either persuasion attended a church anyway. Nevertheless their inherited religion was vehemently defended, often causing a deep chasm between people of the different beliefs.

None of the staff seemed very disturbed, when a conductor entered the staff canteen one day with two black eyes. I heard, through the depot grapevine, that he had entered into a mixed marriage. The conductor's brothers-in-law had beaten him up because they believed he was persuading his wife (their sister) to change her religion to his.

I was also horrified when another colleague, also from a religiously mixed marriage, told me that his six-year-old daughter had died several years earlier but his in-laws had refused to attend the funeral because it wasn't held in their church.

From my agnostic perspective, I thought it was unimportant which religion a person supported. I couldn't understand why a person pouring water over a baby's head in one building in preference to another, could have such far-reaching consequences in that individual's life.

This division between Catholics and Protestants expressed itself in the Glaswegians devotion to the game of football. Protestants supported Glasgow Rangers and Catholics supported Glasgow Celtic. Not being interested in any form of sport at all, I was amazed by the passion this game generated in the local men, and even women.

Anne's father was an extremely zealous Rangers supporter, because he came from a protestant family. Anne told me he had once angrily chased a youth down the road, simply because the boy stood talking to Anne outside their flat wearing a Celtic scarf. I found this tribal warfare quite fascinating. I felt I owed my allegiance to Celtic because I had been christened in a Catholic church, but living in the home of such an ardent Rangers supporter I kept my thoughts to myself. Being English, my opinion was considered inconsequential in these hostilities anyway.

As the damp cold of autumn turned to the biting cold of winter, the shops steadily filled with all the trappings of Christmas. Now that relations between my parents and I had been restored, I went home for the holidays. Everyone made a special effort to get along. I endeavoured to buy extra special gifts for everyone, in an attempt to divert any animosity toward my homecoming.

I was delighted when Gail obviously loved her little pink mini skirt and matching top. She was thrilled that I allowed her to wear it to the school Christmas party, instead of having to wait until Christmas day to open her gift.

I took a number of presents home with me from Anne and her family, not to be opened until Christmas day. When I opened the small, insignificant looking box Mrs Mackie had given me, I found it was not the bottle of cologne I thought it might be, but was in fact a gold watch, which was the highlight of my holiday.

I was eager to get back to Glasgow in order to take part in the New Year celebrations that I had heard the Scots did so well. However, from the time I arrived back on the morning of New Year's Eve, I felt increasingly shivery and ill. Both Anne and her mum were anxious that I would be well enough to go out on this very special night of the year. Mrs Mackie made me stay in bed all day, and plied me with her special flu remedies in the hope that the symptoms might subside before nightfall. Sadly, it became increasingly obvious I was in fact getting worse, not better, so I would have to spend this illustrious occasion at home. I watched in bitter disappointment Anne buoyantly leave the house to meet her friends, so that together they could share in the revelries to mark this most celebrated night of the year.

Mrs Mackie had spent much of the day preparing the feast that would be traditionally eaten immediately after midnight. The table was beautifully laid and took centre place in the living room. Wrapped in a blanket I joined guests Mr and Mrs Gorman, and the rest of the Mackie family to watch the celebrations on television. All the people in the room heartily entered into the festivities as they laughed and sang along with the people on the television. As the clock ticked round to midnight we were all given a drink, ready to toast in the New Year. In unison everyone joined in with the televised count down to the New Year as the final seconds of nineteen sixty-seven ticked away.

However, when midnight finally struck, everyone in the room spontaneously burst into tears, including the austere Mr Mackie. The atmosphere in the room completely changed from one of merriment to great sadness. Everyone was weeping uncontrollably, leaving me totally mystified by this instant change of mood. Seeing the lovely Mrs Mackie crying into a handkerchief made me suddenly feel like an intruder at this clearly very personal time.

When the communal wailing eventually subsided, several wet faces kissed me as everyone began wishing each other a happy New Year. When the earlier jovial atmosphere returned, Mrs Mackie explained to me this was a very nostalgic and poignant time of year for many Scots. Memories of absent friends who had shared previous New Year's celebrations come flooding back to peoples' minds. However I wasn't totally convinced by this explanation. I thought it was more likely to be all the alcohol they had consumed during the evening.

After a short time, Mrs Mackie declared it was time to eat. Everyone moved to the table to enjoy the sumptuous turkey dinner laid before us. Because I felt so unwell I ate very little, but I ate what I could in an attempt to show my appreciation for all the hard work done by Mrs Mackie that day.

After the meal and the washing up was over there was a knock at the door. I was surprised because it was well past midnight. However, no-one else was surprised, in fact they were eager to see who it was. The neighbour came in and wished everyone a hearty "Happy New Year", then gave us all a tot of whisky from the bottle he was carrying. No-one was allowed to refuse, because this was considered bad luck. So even though I disliked the taste of spirits, I took a sip to keep everyone happy.

For good luck to continue for everyone of the household throughout the coming year, a dark haired person with a gift had to be the first to cross the threshold on New Year's Day. It used to be a lump of coal, but these days, more often than not it was a drink from the bottle of spirits they would be carrying. Mr Mackie then returned the gesture, giving the neighbour a tot from one of the many bottles of spirits lined up on the sideboard he had bought for this special occasion. When everyone had finished their drink, the neighbour went off to the next house. Mrs Mackie explained to me, this tradition was known as first footing.

The front door had hardly closed before the next visitor arrived. It continued like that throughout the night. The street thronged with revellers, and the lights in every home continually burned throughout the night. I don't believe I could have enjoyed myself more had I gone out with Anne. But by five o'clock in the morning my strength had finally given out. Disappointed at having to leave the continuing festivities, I retired to bed. Although there was still noisy activity in Mrs Mackie's little living room, I slept through it, having become quite drunk. All the little sips from the many different bottles of alcohol, had taken their toll. Fortunately unlike England at that time, New Year's Day in Scotland was a public holiday. Most people spent it in bed, recovering from the previous night's celebrations.

The friendship that had begun so casually between Anne

and a male colleague in the bus depot was steadily growing into something much deeper. When I returned from my Christmas break, seeing Anne and Sammy together made me realise how serious they were about each other. It was understandable that they enjoyed spending an increased amount of time on their own, as their relationship blossomed.

Sadly, I knew the time had come for me to say goodbye to Scotland. I sent a letter to my mother asking if the invitation she had extended to me at Christmas to come home was still open. I was grateful that it was.

Within days, Anne stood waving goodbye to me from the platform of Glasgow Central station on a cold, early morning in February. Through the window of my carriage I watched her recede into the distance, as the train pulled out of the station to take me back to Birmingham. I knew this was the last time I would ever see her.

I had not been aware of just how much I had grown to love the many different people I had met in and around Glasgow. I knew I would miss Anne, but I was surprised at how intensely I missed other people too. I had been completely baffled by Mrs Mackie's extraordinary kindness and generosity to me, a complete stranger. I was surprised by how much I missed a young married bus conductor called Patrick Waters. He would regularly join me in the staff canteen, where we would solve all the worlds' problems over a mug of tea. He had been so kind to me when I first started working at the depot, understanding how timid and lost this wee English lassie had initially felt in this unfamiliar environment.

My heart was lost to Glasgow and its wonderful people. Over the years that followed, haunting memories have never failed to stir when I unexpectedly hear the sound of a Glaswegian accent.

Chapter 10

Chasing the wind

My cousin Susan was already living back in Birmingham when I returned home from Glasgow. It was good to see her again, even though we had continued to correspond while we had been at opposite ends of the country.

I was curious to meet Barbara, the friend Sue had brought with her from Bognor Regis, who was nineteen years old and a native of that town. They had become friends while working together in a restaurant on Bognor's promenade. I liked her, which was fortunate because we spent a lot of time together, listening to music in my uncle's front room.

As the days became brighter and warmer I became increasingly restless and yearned to get away again. Hoping to recapture some of the excitement I had enjoyed during the previous summer at Bognor Regis, I suggested to Sue and Barbara that we might all work a summer season together. Without hesitation Barbara excitedly agreed. However, now that Sue was settled at home, for her it was out of the question.

Therefore it was only Barbara and I who travelled to Skegness where, several weeks later, we began work at the Butlin's holiday camp. After leaving the train station, we joined the coach sent to carry the latest batch of new recruits back to the camp. I was disappointed to find how far the camp was from the town, unlike the one at Bognor Regis, which had been on the town's doorstep. Nevertheless, I was very impressed to find we were not to be housed in slums as we had the previous year, but was delighted to find the chalet maids had been promoted to live in chalets.

We were eventually led to a chalet that would be our

home for the duration of our employment. It was the same standard single room I had cleaned during last year's summer season, furnished with the same uniform bare essentials, a wardrobe, and chest of draws, bunk bed and sink. Nevertheless, I was so thrilled to be living in a chalet, that I didn't mind when Barbara immediately claimed the top bunk as her own.

I felt rather exposed though when I saw both male and female staff walk along the path, directly outside the window. This was so different from the last camp, when the chalet maids living quarters were totally isolated from all the other members of staff.

After we had finally unpacked, we took an investigative walk around the camp. The first thing we needed to do was to locate the nearest bathing and toilet facilities, because our chalet housed neither. Barbara and I tried to look as inconspicuous as possible as we surveyed the amenities around the site, not wanting the uniformed people we saw to suspect we were new recruits on our first day at camp. The style of buildings, the names of the nightspots and the colour of the chalets were all exactly the same as the camp at Bognor Regis, causing great waves of nostalgia to sweep over me. I wondered if I would enjoy working here as much as I had there.

All staff employed in the same line of work lived together on the same chalet line. It was an impressive sight to see the staff heading for the dining room the next morning, arrayed in their different coloured uniforms. It soon became easy to identify where an employee lived, simply from the uniform they wore.

When we started work, just like the previous year, it gave me a thrill to hear the different accents and to discover where everyone was from. This year the staff seemed to have been gathered from all corners of the British Isles.

It was during this induction Barbara and I discovered our

next door neighbours were Jackie and Anne from Hull. We soon became good friends with them, as well as the girls on the other side of our chalet, Elaine and Pat who had travelled down from Newcastle. During the day the six of us would regularly lie worshiping the sun together on the grass verge outside our row of chalets. Because Skegness town was so far away from the camp, in the evenings we could usually be found visiting any one of the bars on site.

Many staff members were only there to accrue some money so that they could travel to somewhere more exotic. Some spoke of their intention to go fruit picking in Spain and other Mediterranean countries. Others enthused about moving on to live in a Kibbutz in Israel. These conversations were quite intoxicating and caused feelings of restlessness to rise within me yet again.

The idea of moving to Jersey seemed the most attractive to Barbara and me, because unlike other foreign places, a passport wasn't needed. Judging by what we had been told, we wouldn't need very much money either, because we would get immediate employment in any one of the many hotels and restaurants. After considerable discussion, Barbara and I finally decided we would continue the summer season in Jersey.

There were hugs and tears as we said goodbye to people at the camp who had come to feel like old friends, even though we had only known them for a few weeks. We took away with us many addresses, frivolously telling the owners we would write to them as soon as we were settled, although this did not materialise.

After investigating different kinds of transport to get there, we extravagantly decided to fly. So it was with great excitement that we ultimately boarded a plane headed for Jersey. Nevertheless, as the airplane approached the island we became increasingly nervous. Having impetuously embarked upon this new venture, I now wondered if we were doing the right thing.

We were anxious to get to the capital, St Helier, as soon as we could; having been informed that was where the majority of hotels and restaurants were situated for we needed to find accommodation before nightfall.

When we finally arrived in St Helier, we put our suitcases in the coach station's left luggage department, in order to explore the town more freely. I knew I would enjoy living here for this quaint little town was as pretty as we had been led to believe it would be. We noted the grand hotels and restaurants on the seafront, and were excited believing that we might soon be working in one of them.

Walking up the side streets we saw many small houses that had 'rooms vacant' signs displayed in their front windows. Tentatively, knocking on the door of one of these houses, we were pleased when the owner told us we could have one of the available rooms. However, it was free only until the coming weekend, when the boarding house would be full again with holidaymakers.

Anticipating that Barbara and I would have work and lodgings by then, we happily agreed to take the room. However, our confidence immediately evaporated when we told the landlady our reason for being on the island. "There are far too many young people coming over from the mainland looking for jobs," she told us contemptuously, "Most of them end up begging on the streets before being deported back to the mainland."

As we walked back to the coach station to collect our belongings from the left luggage department, the bright sunshine helped to melt some of the gloom that had descended upon us. In our haste to get here, we realised we had brought far too little money.

The next morning we anxiously took the local newspaper we had bought, to an open-air café where we searched through the situations vacant column, over a cup of coffee. The waitress posts only wanted silver service experience; we didn't even know what that meant. Nevertheless, our hopes were raised a little when we read advertisements for chambermaids in the sea front hotels. However, when we eventually found a telephone box to contact the hotels, we looked in utter horror at the scene that greeted us. There was a long queue of young people waiting to use the telephone, each holding a newspaper. They were obviously there for the same purpose as us. When our turn finally came to use the telephone, the vacant posts we had seen advertised in the newspaper had already been filled.

The following day we arrived at the telephone kiosk much earlier, to make sure we were at the head of the queue. However, a long procession had already accumulated when we arrived. Like the day before, the small number of suitable vacancies had already been filled.

Barbara and I both realised that coming here had been reckless. Jersey was not the Utopia we had been led to believe. Seeing the hoards of begging hippies littering the pavements around St Helier, we determined we were not going to become like them. So although both Barbara and I would have liked to stay longer, we knew the sensible thing to do was to return home quickly before our money had completely run out.

Therefore, we bought two tickets for the ferry, leaving for the mainland early next morning. Unlike the flight coming that took less than an hour, the ferry finally docked at Weymouth late in the afternoon, taking nearly all day to get back. Undeterred by our ill-conceived mission to Jersey, we decided to finish the summer by working at a holiday resort in England. I was already acquainted with Great Yarmouth, so that's where Barbara and I decided we would end our journey.

There was no direct route from Weymouth to Great Yarmouth, so we boarded a coach that took us to Victoria coach station in London. From there a second coach would complete the journey to Great Yarmouth. Unfortunately, our coach arrived too late to get the connecting coach; therefore we had to spend the entire night in London waiting for the next coach to depart to the coast the following morning.

We had heard that hippies congregated on Piccadilly Circus at night. Having nothing better to do with our time, we meandered along to see if it was true. It was quite late into the night when we arrived. We found a large number of hippies assembled under the statue of Eros. No one took much notice when Barbara and I took a seat on the steps and even joined in singing the peace and folk songs; we felt very bohemian. Police cars randomly cruised around the area throughout the night, hoping to remove the unwanted transients. However, when a police car was seen, everyone scurried to neighbouring doorways, like insects when a stone is overturned, to hide until the patrol car had gone by.

Finally, feeling weary and hungry we made our way back to Victoria coach station where we found an empty space in the bleak waiting room among the many people also waiting for the new day to begin, in order to be able to complete their journey. After what seemed like an age, having very little sleep, we eventually boarded the coach that would take us to Great Yarmouth.

Later on that day we left Great Yarmouth coach station to search for a cheap boarding house for the night. On finding one we immediately went to bed. We were so exhausted we slept through the afternoon, evening, and continued on until the morning of the following day. We got up to a delicious, hearty English breakfast which we ate with great relish, not knowing when we would eat another meal again.

Rejuvenated by sleep and food, we made our way to the local labour exchange and were sent for an interview at a restaurant near the sea front, which was recruiting waitresses. We were elated when told we could have a trial period starting the very next day, which meant we were going to eat sooner than we had imagined. Giddy with excitement, we used the rest of the day to transfer our luggage from the station to the accommodation provided for the restaurant's staff.

After a sleepless night, we nervously started work early the next morning. Being so near to the promenade, the restaurant was very popular, therefore very busy. No consideration was made for Barbara and me because we were new or inexperienced. The waiters and waitresses regarded no-one in their battle to get their orders to and from the small kitchen hatch; it was every man for himself. This was very different from my previous experience of being a waitress.

The work had been constant and the pace frenzied all day long. However, the fatigue melted into insignificance, when over the free meal provided by the restaurant, Barbara and I counted the tips we had accumulated throughout the day, we were delighted, at what seemed like the small fortune we held in our hands.

While we were still in a state of mild euphoria at the change in our fortunes the Restaurant Manager came over to our table, holding two envelopes containing a day's pay. He told us we were not experienced enough for the restaurant, so our services would not be required. I was horrified as I looked across the table at Barbara, who was staring down at the tablecloth to hide her humiliation. As he walked away he also told us to remove our belongings from the lodgings as soon as possible. We sheepishly left the restaurant, looking straight ahead in order to avoid eye contact with any of the staff, believing they must already have known we were going to be sacked.

As Barbara and I dawdled back to the lodgings we discussed what we should do next, agreeing that for us, the season was finally over. We decided we would spend the winter together somewhere, to wait for next year's holiday season to begin again. We allowed the toss of a coin to decide whether we would go to London, my choice, or Manchester,

Barbara's. I didn't mind too much when the coin ruled we should spend the winter in Manchester.

We got to the train station late in the evening. The man in the ticket office told us there were no trains leaving for Manchester until the next day. With little more than a day's pay in our pockets this meant we would be sleeping rough again. Darkness had fallen when we eventually dragged our luggage onto the beach. At night it was usually littered with lovers and people with nowhere else to go. Tonight the sands were quite empty. After finding a suitable spot, we bedded down for the night, making a bed by using our suitcases as pillows and our thin summer jackets for blankets. We curled up into a ball in an attempt to brace ourselves against the cold, night air, hoping to get some sleep before our journey the next morning.

After a few restless hours, we saw two men walking toward us wielding flashlights. As they came closer, we realised they were policemen. Finally, towering over us they asked what we were doing there. "Actually, we're waiting for a train!" I replied sarcastically, and let Barbara continue the story. To show my displeasure at being disturbed I turned my back to the policemen and returned to the foetal position in order to conserve as much heat as possible. One of the young policemen appeared to have sympathy with our predicament. He told us there were benches in the police station where we could sleep for the rest of the night, if we wished. As they would have moved us on anyway, we had little choice but to take up their offer, so together with our suitcases, we clambered into the back of their police car to be driven to the local police station.

When he had told the duty sergeant why we were there, the kind young policeman directed us to the benches he had told us about. However, although it was warm inside the building it was almost as difficult to sleep as it had been on the beach. At least the sand made a soft bed, unlike these wooden benches. The bright lights of the waiting room were dazzling, and there were periodic bursts of noise coming from behind the desk, jolting us awake each time we drifted off to sleep. Each time I opened my eyes I saw a different person staring at us, making me feel like an animal in a zoo! At an appropriate time we thanked the sergeant for the use of his bench and left the station. Dawn was breaking when we finally arrived at the train station, where we waited for the next train to Manchester...

Chapter 11

A Winter's Tale

A few hours later, we wearily stepped onto the platform of Manchester's Piccadilly station. It was a pleasant, Saturday afternoon in September. The year was 1968; I was just twenty years old. Once the now customary task of handing our suitcases into the left luggage department was completed, we timidly made our way out of the station to explore Manchester's city centre. Parting with any of our severely depleted finances was only done after a great debate, because we had so little money left. Nevertheless, having not eaten since the previous evening, we enthusiastically devoured the cheapest items on the menu of a little back street café.

After our meal, we sat on a bench in a large garden near the station, with the evening newspaper. Scanning the vacant accommodation column, we circled any flats we thought might be suitable for us. After making a number of fruitless phone calls, we eventually managed to secure an interview with a man who had a bed-sitter available in the Longsight district of Manchester. This information meant nothing to us because we were entirely unfamiliar with the city. Nevertheless, we were very grateful that he agreed to interview us the following afternoon.

Barbara and I wandered back to the area where we had previously been sitting, which we later discovered was called Piccadilly gardens. Our intention was to sit here and while away the countless hours until our appointment the next day. However, as the night wore on, we were quite bewildered to find a constant stream of very friendly men approach us for no other apparent reason than to have a chat. A kind man observing this scene came over to inform us the area was frequented by ladies of the night.

"Oh wonderful!" I said to a mortified Barbara. So we periodically went to sit in a nearby café where we shared a long-lasting cup of coffee. From there we would discreetly move onto a different bench, to avoid being accosted by anyone else. At daybreak we meandered around the nearby streets in order to gaze into the shop windows, and kill time with some different scenery before our interview.

Eventually, the long awaited moment arrived for us to meet Mr Sweet, our possible future landlord. Armed with his address and directions to his house, Barbara and I were silent as we travelled toward our destination, not daring to voice the possibility that this man may refuse to accept us as tenants, or what we would do if he did.

We asked the bus conductor to inform us when we approached the road we had written down on a piece of scrap paper. Walking apprehensively down the street we found the house we were looking for. Taking a deep breath, Barbara knocked on the door. From inside the house we heard footsteps getting louder, until a middle-aged Scottish lady finally opened the door. Smiling, she led us into the smart front room. Just as we had made ourselves comfortable on the settee, Mr Sweet walked through the door, giving his wife leave to depart. Barbara and I sat nervously on the edge of the seat, anxiously trying to give the right answers to each question he asked. In conclusion he asked, "Do you do drugs?" to which we answered "No!" in unison. The final question was "Are you on the game?" When I asked him what game did he mean? Shaking his head, he gave a wry smile and told us we could have the room.

Mr Sweet promptly took us to see the accommodation. Parking his car, he very proudly pointed out which of the large Victorian houses in the road he owned, and indicated which house held the vacant bed-sitter. Like all the others in the area, the house looked rather shabby. The tired, peeling paintwork around the deep bay windows looked dingy and in need of urgent repair. It was obvious the house had seen better days. Mr Sweet then led us into the house, through the poorly lit hallway, to view the room.

Once inside the ground floor flat, there was very little space to move. Crammed into the small space were a big old-fashioned double bed and a large antiquated wardrobe also home to the only available drawer for smaller items of clothing. The room resembled a junk shop rather than a furnished bed-sitter. None of this mattered to us; we were so pleased we had somewhere to live. Without hesitation we both agreed we wanted the flat. We slept well that night. To be able to sleep on a bed again was luxury; we didn't even feel the many lumps in the ancient mattress.

Our first Monday morning in Manchester was spent at the local Labour Exchange. We only wanted temporary employment, so we were willing to take any job offered. Happily, we both left the labour exchange clutching a card, with the description of jobs we were to be interviewed for.

The other part of the day was spent in the depressing, smoke-filled atmosphere of the local Social Security office, where we had to wait in endless queues trying to convince different desk clerks our financial need was grave enough to warrant immediate National Assistance support. After waiting around for what seemed hours, we were eventually called by the cashier. With a great sense of relief we were told we were eligible to receive some money, therefore we were not only able to pay our first week's rent, but buy some food too.

Barbara was interviewed for a job in the factory of a company that made cardboard boxes. The man at the Labour Exchange arranged an interview for me at a small firm requiring a clerk in their sales department. It was quite near the flat, so when I was offered the post I could not have been more pleased. Having been accepted by both firms, at the end of the week Barbara and I not only had a flat, but also were gainfully employed. Our plight was over.

Now that he knew we had the means to pay, when Mr Sweet came for the rent at the end of the week, he asked if we would like to have a look at a better flat, in his house next door. Barbara and I both eagerly followed Mr Sweet as he led us into the adjoining house. Expectantly, we climbed the threadbare stair carpet hardly noticing the musty smell that hung in the air. Then we walked along the eerie, dark, shadowy landing past several other doors, to the vacant flat at the front of the house.

Entering the vacant room, we were amazed to see how bright it was, for the sun shone directly into the room through the huge bay window. As the door opened, the first thing we saw was a single bed lying directly ahead. The large headboard partly obscured a high sash window. At the foot of the bed, just inside the door, was a small wardrobe. We were delighted there were two individual beds so we would not have to share one any more. Gazing around the room, we saw the other bed lying along the left hand wall. Hidden behind the large wooden headboard was an electric cooker that fitted neatly into an alcove. In the alcove on the other side of the open fireplace, was a plastic sink unit. The water-heater sitting above it was a very welcome sight, instant hot water was a treat we had recently been denied. Nestled discreetly under the huge bay window, behind a small kitchen table with two wooden dining chairs either side, was an old, wooden sideboard. There were even two easy chairs sitting either side of the fireplace. Though the room had a rather faded appearance, it was still much cosier than where we were at present. Although the rent was higher, without discussion or hesitation, we told Mr Sweet we wanted to have the room, and moved our belongings to our new address immediately.

We soon settled in Manchester, and became familiar with the surrounding area. Barbara and I made it our business to discover the location of Manchester's renowned nightclubs.

However, as good as they were, they couldn't compare to dancing the night away at the Shoreline Club in Bognor Regis.

Our lives continued quite uneventfully for a while, until one sunny, Saturday afternoon. From the commotion that accompanied their arrival, Barbara and I imagined we had been invaded by an army but ultimately there were only five boisterous boys moving into our previous house, next door. They had come to Manchester with the same intention as Barbara and me, which was to explore the famous Manchester nightlife. Discovering they had come from the Butlin's holiday camp at Pwllheli in Wales, led to an immediate rapport between us. We were to discover only three of them were to be our immediate neighbours. Two Welsh guys shared a flat in another of Mr Sweet's houses down the street. However, they spent so much time next door they might as well have shared the rent.

When I heard their strong accent I took an instant dislike to them. The only Welsh people I had previously known were my father and his siblings, for whom I had little affection. Nevertheless, my opinion of the entire nation rapidly changed when Barry and Dai turned out to be the most charming of the whole group. Although both were quite tall, that's where the similarity ended. Dai (Welsh for David) had thick wavy fair hair; he was always smartly dressed and looked somewhat older than his twenty-one years. By contrast, his flat mate Barry was usually attired in a pair of comfy old jeans. His dark, wispy hair always seemed to hang in his eyes. Although he disliked the small gap between his front teeth I thought it attractive. Against my will I grew increasingly fond of him.

Quinney and Ace were friends from Liverpool, and shared the upstairs front room adjoining the one where Barbara and I lived. Neither was known by their proper name. Ace told us he had been known by this nickname since a small child. Quinney's full name was Michael Quinn. They were the shortest of the group, both being around 5ft 7in although

Quinney was slightly taller than his friend. He was slim, wiry, and had short black hair. Even though most of the time he dressed casually in blue jeans and blue denim jacket, he never failed to look neat. Ace was much stockier, and without effort he always managed to maintain a slightly dishevelled appearance, which Barbara and I found quite appealing. He had shoulder length light brown hair and his enormous sideburns almost met at his dimpled chin. Ace's razor sharp wit was evident from the very first time he spoke to us. Although Barbara and I thought he was the best looking of the bunch, he hardly noticed us, for his only interest was in football. So passionate was he about the game and especially his favourite team Everton, he easily became incensed if anyone dared make a disparaging remark about them. His devotion to the club caused merciless provocation by the others, in order to deliberately inflame his fiery temper.

Lastly, Jeff from Humberside lived alone in a small room at the back of the house next door. He was the tallest of the group; over 6 feet, lean with blonde hair. He was quiet and rather aloof, and quite old-fashioned compared to his friends. In fact he seemed so different to the others, I couldn't help wondering why he had joined them in coming to Manchester.

It was great fun having this motley crew live next door. The Manchester nightlife gradually lost its appeal, for the evenings spent watching the small, antiquated television Barbara and I had rented, with Mr Sweet's latest residents was much more fun. We all enjoyed these evenings, which often descended into light-hearted teasing and mirth. No-one wanted to say good night when the evenings came to an end.

Because we became such good friends, we had free access into each other's lodgings. If either happened to run out of a necessary grocery item such as tea or sugar, they would bang on the wall to request it from the neighbours. The commodity would then be unceremoniously flung from one bay window to the other. These were happy days filled with much laughter.

However, as the late summer sun gave way to the chill of autumn, talk of heading back home escalated among the boys. The novelty of bed-sit living began to wane as homesickness grew. Unsurprisingly, it was Jeff from Humberside who was the first one to leave. He had become more and more isolated from the rest of the crowd, so it was easiest for him to say goodbye. It was only a matter of time before the others, one by one, slipped quietly out of our lives.

There was not even enough in Manchester to hold the two Welshmen, despite a romantic connection having grown between Dai and Barbara, and Barry and myself. When the flat next door finally fell silent, that deep sense of loneliness with which I was so well acquainted, came back to torment me once again.

Had we known how bleak the winter months were going to be, Barbara and I might have also been prompted to leave Manchester. As the days grew colder we started to buy coal for the fire, purchased from a little corner shop not far from where we lived. The return journey from these trips always seemed much longer. The heavy load we carried back home seemed to increase with every step. Having the extra burden of buying coal each week taxed our meagre finances. After paying the other necessary bills we were left with very little.

The house I grew up in also had a coal fire, until my father eventually acquired a modern gas fire. My current experience was not nearly as pleasant as those distant childhood memories. I soon discovered that trying to light the coal fire was a very messy and time-consuming business. Even before the attempt began, all the ash from the previous fire had to be cleared away and disposed of. After we had managed to get the fire alight, it seemed like an age before it finally produced any heat. Once we did manage to coax the fire into existence, Barbara and I were forced to continually move our chairs back and forth; when the fire finally roared into life, our chairs were moved back to prevent us from being roasted alive. As the fire died down our chairs were drawn nearer and nearer to the fire to capture the ever decreasing heat. The whole procedure would begin again when more coal was put onto the dying embers. The faded carpet around the hearth was littered with holes and burn marks, to indicate where leaping sparks had landed from the fire. To come home from work tired and hungry to the cold flat, knowing the dreaded task of lighting the fire had to be completed before anything else could be done was very disheartening.

When I awoke on the dark, winter mornings I could easily see the kaleidoscope of patterns Jack Frost had painted on the frozen windows, for there wasn't enough material to close the shabby curtains properly. My feet would often be as cold as ice. Knowing I would be even colder when I got up, I would lie in bed until the last possible moment, before having to get up for work.

It was during these winter months that Barbara and I realised we had mice. Settled in our armchairs to watch the television in the evenings, with only the glow of the fire as light, we would watch them run up and down the inside wall of the fireplace. Every night before we went to bed, we would lay traps, and every morning without fail we would find squashed mice around the room. Using them only once was an unnecessary expense, but we didn't have the stomach to extract the crushed bodies from the traps, so we would throw both trap and mouse onto the fire.

The bathroom was as neglected and decrepit as the rest of the house. The enamel inside the bath had long since perished, but Mr Sweet hadn't thought it necessary to replace. Instead it had been painted; therefore taking a bath was a daunting and unwelcome prospect, followed by the delicate operation of extracting pieces of rust and paint that had managed to remain glued to your skin.

During this period I developed a constant itching between my fingers. It was so severe I scratched my hands until they bled. My local GP prescribed a lotion, telling me to use it after a very hot bath. He did not tell me I had scabies which was caused by a parasite. Neither did he tell me the affliction was extremely contagious or reputed to relate to unclean environments.

Without this information, I ignorantly told everyone in my office of my condition and was greatly alarmed by people's distant attitude towards me. Later in the day, in front of a hushed audience, I was summoned into my manager's office. After some discussion with my boss I was told not to return to work without a doctor's letter confirming the scabies had totally cleared up. I felt so humiliated that I was extremely reluctant to return to the office after I had recovered.

Barbara had happily listened to my many stories of working on the Central SMT buses in Glasgow. Learning that my wages had been a great deal more than our present income she suggested applying to work for one of the bus companies in Manchester. Under the circumstances I willingly agreed.

Together we applied to Salford Bus Corporation and eagerly sent off our application forms. Eventually the long awaited letters arrived, inviting us for interview. Barbara and I were interviewed with a batch of other hopeful recruits and were delighted when we were both offered posts at the same garage, the Weaste bus depot in Pendleton, Salford. Although the depot was way over the other side of Manchester, we soon became used to the long journey to work every day.

When I first entered the garage, the smell of oil and diesel fumes and the sound of buses being revved up getting ready to leave the depot, evoked poignant memories of the depot at Old Kilpatrick in Scotland. Sadly I was not to find the camaraderie here, or the excitement that I had experienced north of the border. Unlike working on the buses in Scotland, which I had found so adventurous, the experience in Salford was familiar and humdrum.

Soon after training, Barbara and I were given our own bus

routes to conduct. My driver, who had been in the job for most of his working life, was a grumpy middle-aged man. He had the rather outdated notion that working on the buses was a man's job. Therefore he was not at all pleased when told his new partner was a young female.

Having nothing at all in common with me, my driver took to staying in his cab during our tea breaks, which I didn't mind at all. I would usually sit curled up on the three-seater bench just inside the lower deck of the bus. Late one evening the bus was sitting at its usual terminus while we took our break in the centre of Manchester. Believing we had plenty of time before setting off on our next trip, I didn't think it necessary to inform my driver I was going to use the nearby public lavatory. When I returned to the terminus, I was horrified to find my bus had disappeared! Seeing an inspector, I ran to tell him the awful news.

"It's just left." He said, calmly.

"But it's gone without me!" I wailed.

"So I see." He said, apparently quite indifferent to my dilemma. He then instructed the crew scheduled to follow our bus to leave a few minutes ahead of time, in order for me to join my bus.

Fortunately, when several perturbed passengers informed my driver there was no one on board conducting, he parked a few miles down the road in the hope that his idiot conductress would eventually appear. After saying goodbye to the other crew, I climbed on board to a round of applause. The passengers thought the event was very exciting, unlike my driver who was not amused at all.

The other time I became unintentionally separated from my bus and driver was during the evening rush hour. The city centre was bustling with people anxious to get home from work. My bus was travelling down Deansgate, one of the busy main streets in the heart of the city. A common practice among the drivers was to flag one of the other buses down for assistance, if they happened to run into any difficulty. The usual cause was simply that their conductor's ticket supply was running low.

I wasn't too anxious when my own ticket supply became severely depleted, for there were many buses around at this busy time of the day. The problem was to decide which of them to borrow from. I pondered on my decision while standing on the platform of my bus waiting for the traffic lights to turn from red to green. I finally decided to go to one of the buses I'd seen stationed at a nearby terminus.

I intended to walk along the nearside of my bus, in order to inform my driver of my plan, for I didn't want him to worry when I wasn't on the bus at our journeys end. However, immediately I stepped off the platform onto the road, the amber light appeared on the traffic lights. I tried to run faster than the lights could change, but before I reached the front of the bus it had started moving forward, as the amber light turned to green. Horrified, I shouted and banged on the side of the bus in an attempt to attract my driver's attention, but to no avail. I stood waving frantically, hoping to attract his attention through his rear view mirror, but I watched my bus disappear into the distance. I felt acutely embarrassed as people turned to stare at me, as I stood in the middle of the street still wearing my heavy ticket machine and money bag.

Wondering what to do next, I decided it was best to proceed toward my mission. After acquiring the necessary tickets, I returned to the place where I had stepped off my bus. Standing on the opposite side of the road I waited for it to reappear. By the time my bus came into view, a long line of people had assembled at the bus stop. When the bus finally stopped in front of me, my bus driver, red faced with rage, yanked open the window of his cab and bellowed,

"Where the f***ing hell have you been!"

"Waiting for a bus," I replied, which caused a ripple of laughter to run down the queue of waiting passengers. I jauntily hopped onto the bus, in an attempt to show the watching onlookers I wasn't embarrassed by the verbal tirade, even though I felt mortified by the whole incident.

Barbara and I both went home for the Christmas holidays. To wake up in my own comfy bed, seeing my sister's golden hair spread across her pillow as she lay sleeping in the bed next to mine was sheer bliss. I listened contentedly to my parents' familiar voices rising from the kitchen below, mingled with the aroma of bacon and eggs. I knew they were sitting at the kitchen table below, eating their English breakfast; a time-honoured tradition they had practised every single Sunday morning as far back as I could remember. It felt so good to be home.

Desperate to know what the future held for me, I asked Lorraine if she would take me to have my cards read by her gran again, which she kindly did. After a cup of tea, Mrs Hughes got the cards out. Shaking her head, she told me she could hardly tell my fortune. The cards said my life was like sand tossed in the wind, which I supposed was true. Sadly they didn't forecast any sign of me settling down in the near future. I was disappointed at the news; it was not what I wanted to hear.

The time to return to Manchester came round all too soon. Being back at home with my family made it very difficult to return to that cold, shabby flat. However, when we got back I found Barbara had the same thoughts I had, so we agreed to move as soon as we could.

We found lodgings with an elderly Irish couple, who lived in a small terraced house just round the corner from our bus depot in Salford. It was wonderful to be able to leave the house just a few minutes before we were due to start work, after previously having to travel so far. As long as Barbara and I conformed to the few rules that we agreed upon, everything was fine. Mrs O'Shea was a sweet lady, who did everything she could to make us comfortable. We were even allowed to watch their television with them if we chose to. Nevertheless after having my own flat, I felt being boarders in someone's house far too restricting. My present existence had become crushingly dull and I wanted to go home.

Barbara's widowed father had re-married and she felt like an intruder in his second family. Whenever I attempted to tell her of my desire to return home Barbara accused me of abandoning her. Returning to Bognor Regis was not an option for her, she lamented. Every time I broached the subject, Barbara would plead with me to stay. Therefore I stopped telling her I was homesick, because it caused so much friction between us. Nevertheless I pined for home.

Eventually I wrote a secret letter to my mum telling her how I felt, and asked if I could come back home. I received a letter quite quickly, informing me both she and my father were agreed that I should return. I was overwhelmed with gratitude and relief.

Telling Barbara my decision was final and irreversible was harrowing. Her resignation of the inevitable was more devastating than the escalating rows of late. Giving my notice to Mrs O'Shea was also distressing. She tried to make me reconsider my decision by telling me they would not be able to advertise for another tenant, because Barbara was still using the room and they really needed the income. Nevertheless, when she could see my mind was made up, she also conceded defeat. I felt so guilty for all the pain I seemed to be causing everyone. However, not everyone was sorry I was leaving Manchester …. my bus driver was delighted!

Barbara had already gone to work when I left the little house for the last time. She didn't want to say goodbye to me, and I didn't blame her. When I first returned to Birmingham I searched the post daily for a letter in her handwriting, hoping she may have forgiven me. Over a period of time I wrote several letters to Barbara, although I never posted any of them. Sadly we never communicated again.

Chapter 12

The theft of innocence

It had been with a warm sense of security that I travelled back to Birmingham, knowing I would not have to return to Manchester again. My coming and going from the family home had by now become routine, therefore although I didn't verbalise any plans to go away again, my parents were aware that this homecoming was again likely to be temporary. My father had conceded defeat in trying to tame his headstrong eldest daughter, so he didn't try any more. My long suffering mother had learned to mediate quickly with individuals in the family before any smouldering resentment could escalate into all out war. So, while I was in residence, a fragile peace prevailed.

It was not long before I found employment at a firm that made baby equipment, known locally as the Dummy Factory. Although the work was repetitive, I enjoyed working there for the radio was played constantly throughout the day on the company's Tannoy system, alleviating the boredom considerably.

Among the teenage girls working at the factory was Liz Josephs who enjoyed my stories of working at the holiday camps. When I told her I hoped to go again, even if alone, she immediately offered to join me. I was delighted.

Jointly, we decided to apply to work at the Butlin's camp at Minehead in Somerset. When we eventually received confirmation that our appointments were secure, it seemed to take forever until the day we finally arrived at the train station in Minehead, eagerly anticipating whatever lay ahead. I was pleased to discover the camp, like Bognor Regis, was situated right next to the town. Therefore, I was quite confident we would enjoy our time here.

Although I had not been to this camp before, as expected, it felt very familiar, for it was practically the same as the others I had seen. After the customary preliminaries, Liz and I were escorted to our chalet. The staff chalets, and the staff dining room, were inside their own enclosure, totally segregated from the holidaymakers' residences and surrounded by a high fence. Our accommodation was on the last row of the staff chalets, overlooking trees and fields, which was very pleasant. Through previous experience I knew everyone else on this row would also be a chalet maid.

When Liz and I started work the next day, although I already knew the routine, I still found it fascinating to hear all the accents from across the country. Not many days passed before new friendships began to form, as everyone became better acquainted. Liz and I made friends with two girls from Swansea in Wales. The pair was quite flamboyant, easily recognisable from afar when wearing their identical, mini, plastic trench coats. Janice's was a dazzling pillar-box red, suiting her dark good looks. Wendy's 'mac' was bright banana yellow, matching her long blonde hair. At five foot one inch she stood just slightly taller than me.

I was amazed to discover a casual acquaintance from home working in one of the camp shops. Faith was a friend of my cousin Sue and had been encouraged by her to get a seasonal job at Butlin's for respite from an unhappy domestic situation. Although Faith was over ten years older than me, meeting at this unlikely place immediately caused a friendship to spring up between us.

This being my third season of cleaning chalets, the work rapidly became tedious. When I told Faith how I felt, she simply suggested I ask to change my job. I applied for a post as a shop assistant and was delighted to find how easily and quickly I was able to swap jobs. I was assigned to the store that sold holiday mementos and trinkets, and luckily worked on the next counter to Faith. The shop was quite quiet for most of the time, so working here was much easier than cleaning chalets.

The manageress, Mrs Daniels, a much older lady and a native of Minehead, wasn't too happy about my new posting. She had conscientiously managed this shop for many years. Her desk was high up on a platform in the centre of the store, from where she could survey everyone and everything that went on. She was unimpressed by staff who didn't take the work seriously, and who had only come here for a good time. People like me.

Minehead was a picturesque little fishing village. It soon became evident the quaint, old-fashioned pub by the harbour was a favourite haunt of many of the camp staff. It was not long before Wendy, Janice Liz and I also became regulars at this lively watering hole, where the latest pop music blared out from a jukebox in a corner of the only room. Although I usually went along to the Pier with Wendy, once inside we often separated in order to mingle with other new friends we had made during the brief period we had worked at the camp. Having discovered Somerset's renowned cheap, very potent, rough cider, commonly known as Scrumpy, at the end of the night we would hunt for each other through the crowd, in order to stagger drunkenly back to the camp together.

The sandy beach was where most of the camps' off duty staff congregated on sunny days; a small group would regularly grow into a large gathering. This was where Janice, Wendy, Liz and I headed during our free time. One afternoon, Wendy and I were at the beach enjoying the summer sun with gathered Butlin's staff. From where we were sun bathing we could easily see the forest covered peninsular that lay beyond the little harbour. I casually commented to anyone who wanted to hear, that since I first arrived I had wanted to explore that far-flung region. One of the assembled male kitchen hands immediately volunteered to go with me, although I didn't really want to at that particular moment, his constant coaxing finally persuaded me to consent. I naively waved goodbye to those gathered on the beach and wearing only flip-flops on my feet, I set off accompanied by this dark, stocky stranger.

After walking for some considerable time we had only just reached the edge of the wood. I realised my desired destination was a great deal further than I had imagined. Feeling extremely weary, the expedition ceased to be any fun, so I suggested we turn back. My almost silent companion proposed we take a rest on the part of the beach we were able to see through the thicket before returning. Without waiting for an answer he swept me up, carried me over the bracken and brambles to a small clump of grass where I was abruptly flung down.

Before I knew what was happening he had knelt across me so that I was unable to move. In silence he unzipped his jeans to expose himself to me. I was suddenly startlingly shocked into reality as I realised what he intended to do. I made a feeble attempt to talk him out of his objective but my stumbling words fell onto deaf ears. As he lay on top of me I could hardly breathe, much less scream. As his open mouth moved all over my face I could smell the pungent odour of stale alcohol on his breath. I desperately tried to struggle free, but the more I struggled, the tighter was his grip on me. As his hands roughly groped inside my tee shirt, unbelievable pain tore through me as I felt him penetrate my body. When he had finished he got up and ran away.

I felt sick to my stomach. Things like this did not happen in real life, only in books or in films. I felt so dirty that I had been used by a complete stranger then tossed aside like a disposable piece of rubbish. I wondered how he could have been so ruthless to have violated me in such a degrading way. I don't know how long I sat holding my knees, rocking backwards and forwards in the foetal position, staring numbly into the horizon, listening to the waves lapping onto the seashore. No wonder he had been so quiet, he must have been planning when to make his move, I thought. I realised it must have been his intention all along to lure me away from the crowd in order to rape me. I hated myself for being so gullible as to have walked away from the protection of the crowd to this lonely isolated place with a man I didn't know.

As though a spell had been broken I was abruptly jolted back to my senses when I realised he could come back at any time. Because of my inappropriate foot wear, I stumbled and fell all along the lonely shingle, as I tried to run back to camp to where I knew I would find safety.

Once inside my chalet I washed all over in an attempt to get rid of the feeling of revulsion and disgust I felt, but it didn't work. When Liz came into the chalet, she was surprised to see me in bed at such an hour. When I told her what had happened, not knowing what else to do Liz ran to fetch Wendy and Janice. They all insisted I tell the police or someone in authority at the camp what had happened, but I didn't want anyone to know, I felt so ashamed. I thought if I remained silent, the whole ugly episode might go away.

The next morning, getting out of bed was quite painful. The reason, I quickly discovered, were the bruises on my body that had now become visible. For moral support, my friends flanked me as I walked into the dining room, for I was afraid I might meet my attacker. Fortunately he was not there. I also feared that it might somehow be visible to the casual onlooker that I had been so callously raped. Surprisingly, no one noticed that I was different from the carefree person I had been yesterday. No-one saw that I had been so viciously robbed of my innocence only to be left with a deep sense of fear and shame, or that a part of me had died.

I bought a penknife that became my constant companion. It was partly for my protection, partly in the hope that I might have the opportunity to use it on my abuser, although that never arose. I saw him once or twice, and then he disappeared for good. The news travelled fast for I heard through the grapevine that he had left the camp having been beaten up for what he did to me. Whether that was true or not; I don't know, but it gave me satisfaction to think that it was.

Days turned into weeks and life continued on in much the same vein as before, except that I began to feel nauseous and my taste in food seemed to change. I refused to believe what my body seemed to be telling me. Nevertheless, encouraged by my friend Faith, I went to the camp surgery where I was given a pregnancy test. Several days later I returned for the result and was told the test had been positive. I was pregnant. Dazed, I walked slowly back to the shop where I worked. During the remainder of the morning I had difficulty serving the small number of customers who came to my counter; my mind just didn't function properly.

When lunch time finally came, I hurried to my chalet. Now feeling totally bereft, after closing the curtains I sat on my bed in the darkened room, gazing at my open penknife. A quiet scream inside told me the only way out of my predicament was to end my life. I took the penknife and walked over to the sink. I held my arm over the bowl to catch the blood I thought would pour out when I cut my wrists. However, I hadn't considered that the blade might be blunt; therefore when I nervously cut into my flesh it left little impression. Although I hacked furiously several times, I was only left with a number of bloodless scratches for my effort.

Disappointed, I ran to the chemist shop to buy some razor blades so that I could do the job properly. Back at my chalet, I hadn't had time to open the pack of blades before there was a knock on the door. My heart pounded as I sat on my bed in silence, hoping the caller would go away. "I know you're in there, I saw you go past my window." the voice said in Wendy's Welsh accent. She knew that today I was going to find out the result of the pregnancy test. My silence must have told her the outcome because she knocked even louder and began shouting for me to open the door. Hearing other voices join hers, I realised a crowd must be gathering, curious to know what the commotion was all about.

"Go away!" I yelled.

"No, let me in!" she insisted, as she continued to bang.

Eventually fearing someone would call Security, I opened the door.

"Well, what do you want?" I asked, returning to the bed.

Wendy came and sat beside me. Without a word she gently opened my clenched fist to find the razor blades I was clutching. In doing so she saw the scratches on my wrist. Yanking my hand away from hers I snapped, "I want you to go."

"How could I leave you in the state you're in?" she said. For several minutes we sat leaning against the concrete wall, silence hung between us. Eventually Wendy broke the silence with, "So it was positive?" I nodded my head reluctantly. By now the panic that gave me the courage to kill myself was subsiding, leaving in its wake an overwhelming sense of despair. I was thankful Wendy didn't feel it necessary to offer any advice. Nevertheless, her quiet presence was a comfort that assured me of her support.

As gossip about my pregnancy spread, I found there was a shift in the way many people behaved toward me. Although some avoided me, not knowing what to say, I found great kindness in the most unlikely quarters. Two Scottish kitchen hands Brad and Davey, regulars at the Pier, who had already become friends of Wendy and mine, appointed themselves as my guardians. My plight seemed to bring out a protective quality in these two Glaswegian hard men, for whenever I was at the pub they were never far from my elbow. On the occasions I went outside for a breath of fresh air I knew Brad, Davey or Wendy would soon follow to see how I was. I found great strength in their friendship

As my position in my parents' affections was precarious at the best of times, I knew I could not ask them for help, confident they would disown me completely if they found out I was pregnant. I knew I could not look after the baby on my own, but nonetheless I still wanted it to have all the things I had no way of giving, so I made the painful decision to have it adopted.

The camp doctor referred me to a local GP who in turn referred me to an adoption agency. The consulting office was in Taunton, one of the larger Somerset towns. The interviewer was professional and detached, only occasionally giving me the courtesy of eye contact. He must have interviewed countless girls in a similar position to me, so why should he care how I felt about giving my baby up? He wanted information about my family; education, social standing, hair and eye colour of the parents and grandparents and so forth, to help match the baby to his or her future parents. When I told him I had no knowledge of the fathers' background because I had been raped, he seemed quite unimpressed by this information. As he led me to the door of his office he told me he would make arrangements for me to go to an unmarried mother's home in the area, where I would stay until after the birth and adoption of the baby.

As I walked out into the bright summer sunshine, the warmth of the sun did nothing to bring to life the deadness I felt inside. Alone in the train carriage on my way back to Minehead, I wept with shame and despair.

My good friend Wendy was anxiously waiting for my return. After recounting to her all the events of the morning, she in turn told me she was going to get a flat near the unmarried mothers' home. Whatever lay ahead for me she would be at my side. I wept again but this time with gratitude for her kindness.

For several weeks I had neglected to write to my mother, my mind being in such turmoil. However, I did write to my sister Gail, secretly explaining to her that I was pregnant and the baby was due to be born in February, so I would not be coming home until the following spring.

The highlight of the day for many of the staff in the store was to see the postman hand Mrs Daniels the post, knowing soon afterwards she would come round to give their mail from home. Seeing the handwriting, I knew the letter in Mrs Daniel's hand was from my mother. As I read it, I let out an involuntary gasp sat down on my stool and cried uncontrollably. Mrs Daniels hurried back and escorted me into the storeroom away from prying eyes where I showed her the letter. Anxious for information about me, my parents had read the letter I had written to my sister stating I was pregnant.

My mother's letter read that although I had previously caused them worry and grief, they never imagined I would sink so low as to bring this shame to their door and were pleased I was not going to return home until everything was over. It was of some consolation to them that the neighbours wouldn't find out about me. Even though there was no trace of sympathy or pity in the letter, I was relieved I would still have somewhere to go when the situation was finally resolved.

Discovering I was pregnant, Mrs Daniels was more kind to me than I could have imagined. Taking it upon herself to look after me, she often invited me round to her house for tea, and we became good friends.

In 1969, abortion was now legal. As I did not comply with the rigorous criteria required by the National Health Service, Faith, told me one of the kitchen hands knew of a private abortion clinic in London. I asked him for the telephone number and promptly arranged a consultation, wanting to be out of this nightmare as soon as possible. I was glad the clinic agreed to do a termination and arranged to pay the large fee in instalments over several years.

It was difficult saying goodbye to the friends who had

been so supportive during the recent harrowing months. Wendy and I pledged to stay in touch, and did for a very long time. Then for the last time I went through Butlin's large iron gates to the waiting taxi that would take me on the first leg of the journey to London, accompanied by my constant companion, my suitcase.

In London I gave another taxi driver the address of where I was to go. Arriving at the clinic, I left the taxi with great reluctance. The inside of the building was very smart and the receptionist very polite. From my seat in the reception area I nervously looked around the room thinking the décor resembled a hotel more than a hospital.

Eventually I was taken to a private room where I was told to undress for the doctor who was coming to examine me. A little later, two more men arrived with a trolley to take me to theatre where I was given an injection that made me sleep. Later, I awoke to find I was in the same room I had been in on my arrival. I was allowed to stay there for the night, to give some time for the effects of the anaesthetic to wear off. After breakfast in bed I got dressed, surprised to find how easily I could do my skirt up. Dragging my suitcase, I left the hospital to cross London in order to get to Euston station for the train going to Birmingham. I was glad I was finally going home.

Arriving at my parents' house, my mother anxiously asked me if I was all right. How could I tell her that I grieved for the baby I had carried so briefly or that I was tormented by guilt for what I had done, so I just told her that I was OK. We both seemed to be at a loss for words, for there didn't seem to be much more to say about the matter. My father made no comment at all. I knew he didn't believe my explanation of what had happened at Minehead and I hated him for it. However, both my parents were relieved that the scandal of their unruly daughter becoming pregnant out of wedlock was not to be exposed.

Chapter 13

Somebody cares

The recent events further eroded relations between my parents and me and by Christmas I had moved out of my parents' home and into a room at the YWCA in the centre of Birmingham. One of the transient residents had travelled from London and was on her own in the city. I happily agreed to accompany her to the city centre nightspots, having progressively lost contact with most of my Birmingham friends. Having nothing at all in common with this new acquaintance it was no great loss when for no reason I knew of, she left the YWCA and abruptly disappeared from my life. However, having become a familiar face at the venues we had frequented, I refused to be deterred by her departure and continued to visit our old haunts alone.

Many of the people I had become friends with also lived on their own. It was common practice for us at weekends, to go to someone's house after the pubs had shut their doors for the night. We would party through to Sunday morning, as few were in a hurry to return to their empty residences. Going to parties every weekend became a routine part of my life.

A short time later I was surprised and greatly delighted to achieve a long held ambition when I was offered a post as a telephonist at the renowned GPO. To be a GPO trained telephonist was very prestigious indeed. Many large organisations refused to employ anyone on their switchboards without this prerequisite.

My first day was quite daunting because I felt so intimidated by this exalted establishment. It was therefore a great relief to find other new recruits were experiencing their first day too. Firstly we were shown around the telephone exchange. It was very exciting to see the army of telephonists assembled at the huge switchboard that snaked around the large room. Each girl clothed with a black plastic headset, was busily answering the flashing lights on the board in front of her. Supervisors sat at regular intervals behind the operators so that they could closely monitor what was going on. I could hardly believe I would soon be part of this illustrious company.

It was not long before the weeks of training were complete. Although I greatly enjoyed the job to begin with, eventually the work grew monotonous, and the customary restlessness set in again. Being aware that I was under the close scrutiny of a formidable supervisor, only enticed me into being mischievous with the girls sitting around me. I didn't care that many of the stuffy supervisors didn't like me. I also ignored the looks of horror when I sometimes turned up for the Saturday morning shift still wearing my hippy clothes, having come to work straight from a party. I did care though, when I was summoned to the Manager's office and told my contract of employment was finally terminated. Although I begged for a second chance and sincerely promised to improve, it was to no avail. They had had enough; I was given one week's notice to leave.

It was very late one Saturday night when, along with some friends, I had been told a party was taking place at a house near the YWCA where I lived. When we failed to locate the venue, I invited my companions back to my room because the hour was so late and the buses had stopped running. It had been my intention for them to quietly while away the hours in comparative comfort until dawn when the buses started running again. Although I knew I was breaking the rules, I thought it would be more pleasant for them to sit in my room than to wander aimlessly around the cold, dark streets of the surrounding area in the early hours of the morning. Regrettably there were too many in my room to successfully keep the noise down, so it was not long before there was a knock on my door. To the amusement of my guests I opened it to find the Manageress standing there head full of rollers, dressed in a pink, quilted housecoat. She was so enraged to see such a large number of unauthorised people of both sexes assembled in my room that her face flushed to the same bright pink of her housecoat. After telling everyone to get out of my room she instructed me to meet her in her office the following afternoon.

I wasn't looking forward to the interview at all and prepared myself for a major dressing down. However the interview turned out to be very brief. This austere woman refused to listen to my explanation of why my room was full of people in the middle of the night. It was evident this meeting had just been a formality. I was told I had until the end of the week to pack my things and leave the premises; the YWCA didn't cater for people like me. It was quite obvious what kind of person she thought I was. I wanted to tell her that she was wrong about me. I wanted to beg her not to throw me out, but I didn't. I knew her mind was made up and nothing I could say would change it.

One of the girls who had been in my room that night offered to let me stay in her bed-sitter until I found somewhere of my own. I gratefully accepted, even though I was totally unfamiliar with the area where she lived. However, now I was unemployed and homeless again, it didn't really matter where I went.

It seemed as though I had been in this situation so many times before. I was becoming sick of the constant cycle of tracking down accommodation and looking for job vacancies in local newspapers. I wondered how I could ever escape the empty existence I felt I led.

It was not long before I found a flat of my own, which had an air of familiarly about it. The small room had the same excessively large, outdated furniture and the customary

Belling cooker that I usually found in these places. The bed-sitters were always furnished with only the barest of essentials, for little consideration seemed to be given to the comfort of the tenant.

Thankfully I was soon employed again, doing shift work at a factory near the flat. I didn't mind the piecework, for it meant if I worked really hard the wages were quite good, so I felt things were looking up again.

One Saturday evening as 1970 was drawing to a close, I was sitting in my usual corner of the popular city centre pub the 'Tavern in the Town,' contentedly surrounded by people I had come to know well. As the evening progressed, people moved around to chat to friends and acquaintances they had not seen all week. A guy I had only previously seen from a distance came to sit next to me. He told me his name was Colin and he was from Dewsbury in West Yorkshire. We chatted easily all evening; he also lived in a bed-sitter that was only a couple of miles away from mine. At the end of the evening I was quite happy to let him take me home. We met every day after that until Christmas, when I moved into his flat.

Colin and I shared many happy times together and we were hardly ever seen apart. No-one had ever been more kind or attentive to me, I loved him very much. Although we often discussed our future, daydreaming about leaving this single room to live in our very own house, we did nothing to make it a reality. Our friends thought we would eventually marry, but deep down I knew I was not enough for him. He always noticed a pretty girl amongst the crowd, even though he told me they meant nothing to him; he was only looking.

Colin's job was to drive a lorry around Warwickshire and Worcestershire, collecting animal skins from abattoirs for a firm that sold the skins onto other companies, who turned them into saleable objects such as rugs or clothing. I often accompanied him on his travels around the beautiful Midlands countryside, having lied to my employer that I was too ill to go to work.

It was very exciting the first time Colin hired a car to take me to his hometown of Dewsbury, and introduced me to his family. It was enlightening to meet his old friends and to see the neighbourhood he had grown up in. However, during the wedding reception of a close friend I became increasingly agitated when Colin left me sitting on my own for some considerable time during the reception. Not knowing anyone else at the wedding I eventually left the hall, intending to hide in the outside toilet until he returned. I was shocked to find him out there, locked in a passionate embrace with one of the bridesmaids! As usual, after a huge row, he won me round, but this incident only added further to my feelings of insecurity about our relationship.

While we were out driving during another visit to Dewsbury, we noticed a girl standing at a bus stop. Recognising Colin, a big smile spread across her face so he stopped to offer her a lift. After scrambling into the car she introduced herself to me, telling me her name was Christine and that she was an old friend of Colin's. Then followed a conversation between them about mutual friends they had not seen for a while. When we arrived at Christine's destination she asked Colin round to her house that same afternoon to continue the conversation. When he agreed to go, I was determined to go with him for Christine was young and attractive, and I knew Colin.

Fortunately my earlier concerns were unfounded. Arriving at Christine's house we were led into the living room. An open Bible lay on the chair where she had been sitting. In an attempt to impress Colin's friend, I told her I had been religious when I was a child. She laughingly told me that she wasn't religious, explaining that being religious means having to live by a set of rules. "However, I am a Christian" she added "and I do have a relationship with Jesus." Although

Colin and Christine were keen to pursue their earlier conversation, it was difficult for the discussion to gather much momentum. Intrigued by what she had said I kept interrupting with questions about her faith. By the time we left her house I felt so enthused by what I had heard I insisted Colin take me to church when we got home.

Several days after we returned home from Dewsbury, a letter arrived from Christine with the address of a church she recommended. However the desire to go to church had already worn off. The church was too far from our flat anyway, so I threw the letter in the bin and discarded any more thoughts on the matter.

I believed the increasing restlessness I felt would go away if Colin and I got married. However, he was quite content to go on living together in the little flat. We seemed to lurch from one row to another as our relationship slowly deteriorated. Finally, after giving him several ultimatums, I moved out of the flat, hoping it would make him see how much he needed me. Lamentably, moving out did nothing to enhance our relationship at all.

We tried to soldier on for a while. Still together much of the time, only now we had two lots of rent to pay instead of one, so we had less money than ever. Ultimately, we both agreed it would be better for us both to part. During our last night together we lay weeping in each others arms, knowing that although we loved each other, it seemed our future was not to be together.

Not many weeks had passed when Colin brought a new girlfriend to the Tavern. The pain I felt seeing him with someone else was unbearable. From that time on we hardly spoke to each other. However, when across the crowded Tavern Colin's eyes deliberately met and held mine, volumes of words passed between us. I had thought I would be happy to be free but I had never felt more miserable. Although my heart was breaking, I was determined to show him I didn't care anymore even though I could not believe it was really over between us.

It is surprising how lonely a person can feel, even when surrounded by friends. I felt so lost and alone I would often go home from work on the early shift, which ended at two o'clock in the afternoon and go straight to bed. I would stay there right through to the next morning, when necessity forced me to get up to go to work again. While working on the afternoon shift, I would lie curled up in my bed in the morning for as long as possible, having no desire to get up until it was absolutely necessary to go to work. I was slowly sliding down into a deep well of despair, with no apparent way of climbing back up again.

After saying goodbye to my family at the end of a visit one evening, I was surprised when my father followed me out of the house in order to speak to me alone. I knew my parents were concerned about how morose I was becoming, nevertheless I hardly expected to hear my father invite me to live back home. I was warmed by the genuine concern I saw in his face and was very grateful for his invitation, which I duly accepted.

During my long bus journey back across the city to my bed-sitter I thought about my decision to return home, remembering the rows and arguments of the past. However I knew that living with these it would be better than the lonely desperation I was currently residing in.

My sister's dismay that I had moved back home before the week was out was evident. Now aged eighteen, she didn't appreciate having to share her personalised bedroom with me yet again. Although both my siblings did little to hide their irritation that this cuckoo had returned to the nest, I didn't care. The feelings of despair that had recently overwhelmed me were less intense by having people around me.

I terminated my employment at the factory, because the journey was too far to travel from my parents' house.

Fortunately however, I was soon gainfully employed again, wrapping cheese and cooked meats in the basement of a local supermarket.

As Christmas fast approached, one evening I happened to be sitting at the back of a bus travelling into Birmingham, on my way to The Tavern in the Town. A young, hippy looking guy around my age came to sit on the side bench in front of me. When he began to talk to me I was quite happy to engage in conversation with him to reduce the boredom of the long journey. Eventually he asked me if I believed in God.

Without hesitating, I said "Yes I do."

He inquired further, asking if I believed in Jesus Christ.

After giving it some thought, I eventually replied, "Yes, I suppose so."

When he asked if I went to church, I answered rather sharply, "No! If I need to pray I can do it at home just as well as I can in a church."

Without seeming phased by my abrupt manner he said he agreed, as he cheerfully stood up to get off the bus. Pointing across the road he added, "If ever you did decide to go to church, there's a good one just over there. It's full of young people and God goes there too." With that he walked down the aisle and got off the bus. I watched him run across the road and disappear into the night, straining my eyes in an attempt to see the church I knew he was going to.

Christmas was a joyless time. Seeing the hustle and bustle of people doing their Christmas shopping in the over-crowded stores seemed so pointless; even the festive lights and decorations served only to magnify my loneliness.

On Boxing Day evening I attended the Tavern. At closing time, as usual, with the crowd I mixed with, we descended upon Mickey Treadwell's house which was now a favourite rendezvous. He lived in a little terraced house, hidden behind a block of run-down shops in an inner city suburb. I was already quite drunk when I arrived; as the night progressed I became even drunker.

Amongst the crowd were Colin and his girl friend. When she disappeared from his side for a moment, I staggered over to him and asked if he had ever loved me. "Yes once" he told me coldly, "but I don't any more." When I returned to my seat I sat brooding over his words. I returned to him, and impulsively poured the entire contents of the pint of cider I was holding, over his head. Colin's girlfriend, now seated back in her chair, screamed because she too had been soaked in the process. I smugly went back and draped myself over my chair as if nothing had happened.

After consoling his girlfriend, Colin came over and sharply yanked at my hair so that he could have a face to face confrontation with me. The cider from his wet hair, dripped into my eyes and down my face as he stood directly over me. In his temper he swore at me calling me obscene names. Not to be outdone, I returned his anger with more and louder profanities. To stop me shouting, I felt the soft flesh of his forearm in my mouth. I bit it as hard as I could. The next thing I knew I felt his other arm under my legs to lift me by my hair, from my seat. He took me kicking and screaming down the hall, from where he unceremoniously threw me outside onto the street. He then went back into the house, slamming the door behind him.

Standing alone in the darkness, remorse filled my mind as I realised that I had finally destroyed any lingering hope that one day Colin and I might rebuild our relationship. The street was quiet now but during the day it was busy and bustling with people and traffic. Without him in my life I did not want to live. I went over and lay down in the middle of the road, hoping a vehicle must soon come along to finish my misery once and for all. I waited for what seemed like an eternity, but it was in the early hours of the morning during the Christmas holidays and the roads were empty!

Suddenly, I felt a hand under my arm. Opening my eyes, I

saw it was Colin who lifted me from the road and took me back to the pavement. Leaning against the wall of the building we had come out of, he drew me close to him. Melting into his arms I clung to him as one who was drowning would cling to a raft. Sobbing uncontrollably I wailed, "Oh Colin, I'm so sorry." At that moment Lynn, his girlfriend, appeared, and seeing us entwined burst into tears. He walked over to her; she was his first priority. "It's OK this means nothing," I said ruefully to her. At my request Colin went inside the house to get my handbag. I wanted to leave without anyone seeing the dismal state I was in. As I walked away, I turned to see Colin and Lynn walk hand in hand back into the house.

Having previously hitch-hiked around the country without coming to any harm, I held my thumb out to passing cars as I proceeded toward Birmingham, hoping I would not have to walk the entire fifteen or so miles back to my parents' house. Eventually a car did stop, the driver seeing what a drunken, tear sodden mess I was, took pity on me. He must have been an angel, for he gallantly drove me right across the city to deposit me safely right outside my parent's door.

Chapter 14

Colliding with destiny

To wake up the next morning nestled in my own warm bed at home, was something of a relief. Nevertheless, as I slowly emerged from sleep, the pain I felt in my head from drinking too much alcohol and from having my hair dragged out by the roots, was nothing compared to the pain I felt in my heart. The knowledge that I had decimated my relationship with Colin and that now we would never be together was almost too much to bear. I wouldn't blame any of my friends either if they refused to speak to me again for the exhibition I had made of myself at Mickey Treadwell's house. I felt so ashamed I thought I could never walk into the Tavern again. It wasn't the first time I had been the worst for drink, my friends would often tease me about my conduct, but as my memory of the occasion would often be patchy, I had no way of knowing how far they had stretched the truth. However, this time I could not blot out the events of the previous night, as much as I tried. I remembered every degrading moment.

Because of my misery, I cast a cloud over the entire festive season for my family. I was in tears for most of the time over the next few weeks. Eventually my father's patience wore thin for he was unable to understand why I cried over the least little thing.

In a vain attempt to cheer me up, my sister invited me to accompany her and her friend to welcome in the New Year at a city centre nightclub. I went along but sadly, I was so depressed I succeeded in completely ruining their planned revelry. During the evening I met a couple of girls who had once also frequented the Tavern in the Town but had moved on to other city centre nightspots. We spent ages catching up with mutual gossip, to the relief of my sister and her friend who were quite happy to abandon me. Hearing the news that Colin and I had finished, my old friends kindly invited me to join them at their recently discovered venues. I readily accepted, relieved that my social life had not totally collapsed after all.

Through the rekindling of these friendships I was later introduced to an array of new pubs and new people, but somehow the taste for it was gone; yet the random conversation I had with the hippy guy before Christmas frequently invaded my mind. I became so curious about the church he mentioned that I even broke a bus journey to look at the notice board, in order to find out what time the services were. Finally, I decided to attend, just once.

I arrived at the church one Sunday evening just before the service was due to start. I had imagined there would only be a few solitary people scattered around the hall. However, I was surprised to find the small church was buzzing with excitement and overflowing with people. In fact there was only one seat still available, and to my horror it was on the front row! I felt very conspicuous following an usher to the vacant seat as I strutted down the aisle, my favourite maroon, military style coat sweeping around my ankles. Once I was seated I gazed around the room, feeling like a spectator in this totally alien environment. Fortunately, the service began almost immediately, alleviating my discomfort considerably.

I found the melodious singing of the male-voice choir very enjoyable, as I did other items on the programme. To celebrate the opening of a recently built wing, a well-known guest speaker called Percy Brewster had been invited. When the minister had finished preaching, he asked people in the congregation who wanted to give their lives to Jesus to raise their hand, so that he could pray for them. Copying everyone else I bowed my head and heard him count a number of hands that had been raised around the room. After a short silence he said, "There is someone here who used to know the Lord a long time ago. You've tasted all the fruits of the world, now the Lord is calling you back." Immediately in my mind, I was back to the day I walked down the hill near my home with Mrs Andrews, my old Sunday school teacher. I was eleven years old again, hearing her confidently say, "One day you'll be back. You may be a mother or even a grandmother, but you will be back." Knowing without a doubt I was the person he was talking about, on the 9th of January 1972 I also raised my hand and gave my life back to Jesus, just as Mrs Andrews had foretold I would. At the end of the service I wove my way around the groups of people that had quickly gathered, to make my way to the door.

Stepping outside into the cold night air, instead of heading for home I went to one of the pubs in Birmingham to meet my recently re-discovered friends. During the journey I reflected on the events of the previous hour or two. It felt like a great weight had lifted from my shoulders for I felt as though I had finally found the elusive piece of jigsaw puzzle that seemed to have been lost from my life for so long. Going to church hadn't been the ordeal I had expected it to be; in fact it had been such a pleasant experience I decided to go back the next week. When I got to the pub that evening I wasn't even embarrassed to tell my friends where I had been and talked enthusiastically about all that had taken place. I did not realise I had embarked upon my life's greatest adventure and nothing would ever be quite the same again. I did go back to the Tavern a number of times, and was pleased by the welcome I received from my old friends. It was as though the humiliating episode at the Boxing Day party never happened. I was taken aback by some of the attitudes I encountered when I told them of my newfound faith in God. I mistakenly believed they would be as excited as I was when I told them I had discovered that God was real! Most were indifferent to my news, others were simply amused. One friend told me,

"You've just changed one god for another, that's all." I reflected on that, and concluded it was probably true. However, although I couldn't explain it I knew I had found something I had lost a long time ago. Once again I felt the joy that Pilgrim had when his burdens rolled away at the cross. Generally the consensus of opinion among my friends at the Tavern regarding my recent conversion was that finishing with Colin had really messed with my head! Most of my friends were much more forgiving of my drunken exhibition at the party than of my becoming a 'born again Christian'.

When I told my family I had become a Christian, my father gave a quiet, exasperated groan in response to my latest fad. My sister told me, "Everyone goes through a religious phase at some point in their lives," and predicted that I would loose interest in about six months. However, contrary to my sister's prediction I did not lose interest, but steadily fell deeper in love with Jesus as my knowledge of Him grew. I instantly lost the desire to get drunk to oblivion. In fact I steadily lost the desire to go to places that had once held such fascination for me. After several months of pub-crawling around these newly discovered venues, I finally told my friends goodbye. They were not entirely surprised, for my recent change of heart had been quite evident to them.

At the end of the evening I left the pub to walk down the busy street to get the bus home for the last time. As I approached the junction with the road the Tavern was on, I glanced down to see if I recognised anyone coming out of my beloved old haunt. Seeing a man in the distance wearing a familiar white Afghan coat, my heart lurched for I knew the couple walking arm in arm towards me were Colin and Lynn. We reached the junction simultaneously, and having not met since the night of the party, we exchanged superficial pleasantries as we walked toward our required bus stops together. When we arrived at Colin and Lynn's bus stop I continued to walk on alone. As much as I wanted to, I refused to turn my head for just one last look at the man I loved more than anyone else in the world, even though I knew it was probably the last time I would ever see him.

Having slept squeezed together with Colin in a single bed for over a year I felt lost in the little bed I now occupied at my parents' house. I ached for Colin almost more than I could bear and wondered if anyone else would ever take his place. It seemed impossible to think I could ever love anyone else as much as I had loved him.

However, soon after I became a Christian I discovered a verse in the Bible that felt like I had found hidden treasure. It read, "Delight yourself in the Lord and He will give you the desires of your heart." Psalm 37:4. Wealth or riches was not what I craved; just someone who would love me for ever, someone who having only me would be enough for him. It seemed impossible.

My first Christmas that I believed in Jesus was almost as miserable as the previous one had been. During the early evening on Christmas day I answered the telephone to hear the voice of a friend from the church I was now attending, inviting me round to her house for the evening. I declined the offer because I had been lounging around in my pyjamas all day and couldn't be bothered to get changed. After a brief conversation, for no apparent reason, she said, "Sandie, God will give you the desires of your heart!" I instantly wanted to burst into tears but didn't know why! I could not concentrate when I returned to my chair to watch TV. I wondered how my friend had known that I had taken that particular verse of scripture to my heart. A spring of joy began to bubble up inside me. I didn't understand how, but I knew with a certainty that one day God would indeed give me the desires of my heart and I would surely find true love.

I expected the arrival of my husband to be quite imminent after that exchange. Nevertheless I waited and waited and prayed and prayed. Month after month went by without his arrival. Another friend gave me a book entitled '100 promises of God.' So in case God had forgotten I reminded Him of all of them, but still nothing happened. As the next Christmas approached with no prospect of a husband in sight, I tried a different tactic. I told God that if I didn't meet anyone within the year I would leave the church and return to my old life style! This obviously didn't scare God at all, because the following Christmas came and went and I was still on my own. Having at the time, an immature understanding of God I decided to try reverse psychology and informed Him that I didn't want to get married any more, naively hoping this might quickly produce a husband. However, that didn't work either; I still remained alone. I was learning there was nothing I could say or do to rush God. I just had to believe that what He promised He would do, and to wait patiently.

Remarkably, since I had become a believer the atmosphere at home, although not perfect, was greatly improved. The game of trying to aggravate me gradually lost its appeal for my little sister and brother because I was becoming much harder to provoke. Even the arguments with my father seemed to be less frequent. I was forbidden by him to speak about anything that happened at the church, but I was so excited by things I was discovering in the bible I wanted everyone to know about them too, especially my family. Yet I slowly realised not everyone wanted to know, my father certainly didn't!

Some time later I started attending a mid week meeting provided for the younger members of the church. At the bus stop afterwards I often noticed a girl who also attended. Anne Maurice, who was five years younger than me, was as quiet and timid as a mouse. She couldn't have been more different from me for I was bubbly, chatty and liked to give the appearance of being very sure of myself, although I was not. Nevertheless, we were both new Christians and became good friends. At the end of the summer, Sue Beck a long-standing member of the church, returned home from working a 'summer season' at a coastal hotel. She was very different again from either Anne or me, but a similar age and a car owner. As she was happy to ferry Anne and me to different social events held by the various churches across the city, very soon this unlikely trio became inseparable.

The minister of the little church was a young Welshman called Alan Capel. A slender, handsome and very charismatic man also blessed with a stereotypical, beautiful Welsh singing voice. When he sang a solo it was always followed by rapturous applause from the clearly devoted congregation. Often the church was so crowded, the young people were asked to give up their seats to sit on the platform behind the minister, in order to make more room in the auditorium for the expanding congregation.

Being new to the church, when Alan announced to the hushed assembly he was going to live in Canada, I did not understand why people were so distraught by the unexpected news. But having pastored these people so caringly for a number of years, it was evident how highly they regarded him.

Following the departure of Alan Capel, weeks turned into months before a new minister was appointed. The situation became desperate as the congregation steadily diminished in number to the point that it was no longer necessary for the young people to sit on the platform any longer. Therefore everyone was greatly relieved when another young Pastor was finally appointed. His name was Tony Chamberlain and although he was not as charismatic as Alan Capel he was an undeniably likeable man, and a compassionate minister.

Soon after his arrival Tony fulfilled a longstanding commitment to his previous church by taking their youth away on a weekend break. There were still a number of places available so some of the young people from our church, including Anne, Sue and myself went too. It was great fun meeting those from the other church and everyone who attended had a really good time. However, while there I had a rather curious experience. Anne and Sue decided to take a walk after Sunday lunch before we returned home, and I went for a lie down on my bunk bed where I promptly fell asleep. When my friends returned to the lodgings Sue proceeded to read to Anne some of the poetry she had written. Suspecting I was likely to ridicule her efforts, I heard Sue quietly tell Anne to promise not to tell me what she had written. I struggled desperately to tell them I could hear their conversation, but as much as I tried, I could not move my body. Nightmares had been a part of my life for as long as I could remember. I had had this particular experience many times before, but had imagined it was simply another nightmare. Now I realised that although it felt like I was asleep I was not actually dreaming, for I was fully conscious of what was going on around me. Eventually with great effort I was able to move my body as if coming round from sleep. I tried hard to put the incident behind me even though the experience had filled me with fear.

He had only pastored at the church for a short time, but sadly the following year Tony and his wife moved on. This time he was replaced surprisingly quickly by David Woodfield who took up his Pastorate on the 4th February 1974, bringing his attractive Swiss wife Pia, their two small children Cordelia and Mark and a great musical ability with him. Pastor Woodfield was quite different from the previous pastors I had known. Initially I thought he seemed quite aloof and distant for he exuded a quiet, dignified air of authority, which I found somewhat intimidating. However, it soon became evident that David Woodfield was very humorous with a great sense of fun, which caused the youth ministry to flourish again under his leadership.

Soon after David arrived he announced he was going to organise a youth choir which most of the youth joined. A collective decision was made to call the group Revelation and rehearsals took place each week after the Sunday evening service. Although we were very serious about the choir it was also a great social event where we had a lot of fun, occasionally to the point that Pastor Woodfield became exasperated when there was too much hilarity and too little concentration. When he finally felt we were ready to go public, a bale of blue flowered fabric was purchased and from it each girl made a dress of her own choosing, to ensure individuality as well as uniformity. As time went by, our choir became increasingly well known. We were invited to sing at venues all around the country, travelling by coach as far north as Newcastle and as far south as London and the Home Counties. However the majority of engagements were around Birmingham and the West Midlands. During the programme, Pastor Woodfield frequently called upon individuals in the choir to tell how they had become a Christian. I was often called upon to tell my story, which I enjoyed very much because I loved to tell people how I had come to have a faith in God. This was my first experience of public speaking.

Another challenge was the length of time I now managed to hold down a job. Several months after I became a Christian I changed my role from wrapping cooked meat in the bowels of a local supermarket to that of working at a local factory that made plastic hospital equipment. I would often gaze idly around as I added my component to the plastic tubing moving down one of the three large conveyor belts, in the main factory. The clothing worn by everyone on the shop floor was to ensure no stray hair could make its way into the sterile merchandise. However, the rows and rows of women dressed in their matching white overalls and peaked caps reminded me of the rows of cabbages on my father's allotment. I wondered how long I would be planted in this factory, gloomily imagining it would be forever. Although ultimately it turned out to be for four years, the longest I had ever been employed by a single firm. As I daydreamed to alleviate the boredom, I would often imagine myself in some far-flung place of the world, doing some magnificent work for the Lord. One day, sitting at my usual position at the conveyor belt, mentally trekking around the world, a renegade thought passed through my mind, "If you were to do anything at all for the Lord, first you would need to go to Bible College." I wondered "Wherever did that come from?" and felt like laughing out loud at such a preposterous idea, for I believed I was neither clever nor holy enough for such a place. Although I tried to put the idea out of my head, the thought kept popping into my mind until eventually it didn't seem quite so ridiculous in fact the thought grew into a desire.

I was surprised that my friend Anne didn't scoff when I confided to her that I had been thinking of going to Bible College. In fact she was very encouraging and advised me to discuss the matter with Pastor Woodfield. This horrified me because I was sure he would dismiss the idea completely or even worse laugh at my aspirations. However, one Saturday a short time later, the choir and other members of the church were congregated in a small village just outside Birmingham to give out flyers advertising a forthcoming concert. Coincidently, David Woodfield and I happened to be walking down a road together and as we walked, we made the predictably light conversation that two virtual strangers might make. I was eager to take this unexpected opportunity to informally ask him his opinion about my studying theology. Before I had chance to steer the conversation around to my intended subject, he asked, "When were you thinking of going to Bible college?" I was so taken aback that he had pre-empted my words I could hardly speak, and spluttered "Actually, I have been thinking about it." Amused that I had been stunned into silence by my complete astonishment, he told me to ring him later to make an appointment so that we could discuss the matter. During our subsequent meeting I asked him how he knew I had been thinking about going to Bible College. He told me he didn't. "The question just came into my head, so I said it. God does that sometimes, to confirm that the desire a person may have actually came from God." David Woodfield turned out to be more supportive than I could have dared hope. He not only helped me to decide which college I should apply to but was also a great asset in helping to obtain a grant from the City Council in order to help fund my future education.

Eventually I was interviewed by Mr Wesley Gilpin, principal of the Elim Bible College situated in the little village of Capel, nestling in the beautiful Surrey countryside. Before the end of the summer I was delighted to receive confirmation that I had been accepted as a student. Although eager to begin my training I would have to wait nearly a whole year.

Coinciding with the news that I had been accepted by the college, the night terrors I was already familiar with steadily increased. This fleeting paralysis I had previously experienced escalated until it happened almost every night. So much so that I was terrified to go to sleep in case I didn't wake up again. During the hours of daylight I would give myself a good ticking off for being so ridiculous, but at nightfall a feeling of great dread would descend upon me as the clock ticked round to bedtime. I would often leave the bedroom light on all night because I was so afraid of the dark. Regularly, from inside my paralysed body, I would pray or sing songs about Jesus, in an attempt to ward off the ever encroaching evil I sensed was in the room. When I did eventually manage to rouse myself from sleep, my whole body would be damp with perspiration from fear and the effort of trying to wake up. In desperation I finally went to see Pastor Woodfield, in the hope he might make some sense out of what was happening to me. During our conversation he asked me about my past. It was through these questions I realised I hadn't had a nightmare prior to playing with a Ouija board when a teenager. He pointed out that through my previous naïve flirtation with the occult; I had unwittingly opened my life to dark spiritual forces. Now that I was walking with God, the devil was using this open door to disrupt my life as much as possible. Led by Pastor Woodfield I renounced every drug I could remember taking, and every means of fortune telling I had used to try to see into my future. I even renounced the newspaper horoscopes I had once read avidly. When finished, Pastor Woodfield prayed a simple prayer and commanded anything that was not of God to leave me, and then he asked God to fill me with His Spirit just like it says in Acts 2:3 in the bible. There was no drama and I didn't feel any different, yet from that day on I never had another nightmare. Neither was I ever again afraid of the dark or disturbed by things that go 'bump in the night'.

Chapter 15

Heaven on earth

From the beginning of 1975 our Pastor was becoming increasingly dissatisfied with the spiritual climate of the church, so he invited any who wanted to join him, to a special late night prayer meeting he was going to hold on the last Friday of each month. Chairs were taken to the front of the church, where a circle of people would sit and pray. There was no organised programme; those who attended would just sing and worship and seek God. These were joyous meetings. An air of expectancy grew as the awareness of the presence God gradually increased in the meetings.

Ed Miller an American, who had spent many years as a missionary in the Argentine was the guest speaker on Sunday evening 13th of July 1975. The congregation waited expectantly to hear what he was going to say. When Ed Miller got up to speak, he told the story of how he had pastored a small church for a number of years when he first went to Argentina. His small flock was quite unresponsive to anything he tried to do; so in utter desperation he finally cried out for God to do something with these people. God spoke to Pastor Miller and told him to call his meagre congregation to a week of prayer, which he did. We were told that during most of the meetings the congregation sat in awkward silence. At the end of each evening Ed Miller asked the people if they felt God had said anything to any of them. There was no response at all at the end of the first meeting. When the same thing happened at the end of the second evening he pleaded with his congregation to share if anyone had even a suspicion that God may have spoken to them. One woman said she thought God may have spoken to her, but refused to divulge what it was.

The same thing happened on the third night when the same woman said again she thought God may have spoken to her. After much cajoling she eventually told Pastor Miller she believed God wanted her to tap on the table, but refused to do such a silly thing. This happened every night and on the final night of prayer this disheartened Pastor instructed the congregation to walk around the table and for each to tap on it in turn. When this woman's turn came to tap on the table every person in the room was "filled with the Holy Spirit and began to speak in other tongues" just as happened in the book of Acts in the bible. This seemingly insignificant step of obedience was the spark that ignited the fires of revival that raged across the Argentine for many following decades. Thousands of people gave their lives to Christ and the churches began to fill across the nation and beyond as people rushed to see this spectacular phenomenon.

Following this inspiring account of the origins of the Argentinean revival, David Woodfield invited Ed Miller to lead the worship. We repeated hymns and choruses many more times than we were used to. We sang the chorus "The Lord thy God in the midst of thee is mighty" so many times, I became quite exasperated. However, eventually the truth of these words seemed to reverberate throughout my whole being and, like hearing the sound of a train in the distance getting louder and louder, I began to faintly hear the sound of a language that I had never learned in my head. It became louder and louder until I could no longer hold the unknown language inside and the words poured out of my mouth exactly as described in the book of John, 'Out of my inner most being flowed rivers of Living Water,' as the power of the Holy Spirit surged through me like an electrical current. I opened my eyes to see my raised hands were shaking like leaves in a thunderstorm. As I stood worshiping God I felt so euphoric I was hardly aware of anything else that was going on around me. It was as though an invisible Tsunami had swept through the church, leaving a glorious devastation in its wake. People were spontaneously leaving their seats to kneel at the front of the church where they wept openly. This must have been an echo of what happened in Argentina.

It was quite late when the service finally ended, nevertheless the young people still met at Pastor Woodfield's house as usual. We were delighted to have the privilege of being joined by Ed Miller. Everyone sat round him as he happily recounted to his captivated audience many miracles God had done in the Argentine. This fount of knowledge did not tire of answering the innumerable and diverse questions that were put to him by his listeners. I sheepishly asked, "If you were the lowest person in Heaven do you think God would like you as much as everyone else?" secretly believing that place must be reserved for me. He must have known the reason for my question, for his kind eyes looked straight into mine as he said, "My dear, the lowest place in Heaven is a million times better than the highest place in Hell."

After this extraordinary divine manifestation Pastor Woodfield was perplexed to know what to do next with the church services. So he informed the congregation he would open the church the following evening for an informal meeting for anyone who wished to come back. He was amazed to find that nearly the entire church turned up, for so many wanted to be where the presence of God still seemed to saturate the air. Night after night the little building was filled with people, as story after story was told of what had happened to individuals because of that extraordinary Sunday evening service. There was resounding laughter when one man told the congregation that he had been so disgusted at the noise and seeming chaos he had thrown his hymn book down on his seat with the intention of leaving the church, instead he found himself weeping at the altar. The congregation also giggled when a newly married young woman testified that she had been baptised in the Spirit during the meeting. Every time she spoke after the service the words came out in an unknown language so powerful was the experience. She even had difficulty asking her husband what he wanted for his supper! Every evening, one particular man patiently waited in the queue for his turn to tell the congregation of his experience that night. However, as soon as he attempted to speak big tears rolled down his face and he just wept into his handkerchief. A few weeks later after the euphoria had lessened he explained that he was so overwhelmed with the goodness of God that he cried continually for the entire week.

Although the services eventually returned to their usual timetable, there still continued to be an almost tangible presence of God in the building. People were so eager to be at church that many arrived up to an hour before the meetings began, just to sit in the atmosphere. It felt as though we had touched Heaven as the Glory of God seemed to come down when we rose up in worship. With rivers of tears flowing down my face, within my spirit, I would gaze in wonder and awe at the splendour of the Lord as I soared to realms no chemically induced highs could take me. There was such a liberty in the services no one took exception to anything unusual that took place. Seeing children pray for one another to receive the baptism of the Spirit was commonplace. When even staid long standing Christians, who had been in the church for many years, spontaneously and uninhibitedly danced for joy before the Lord, not an eyebrow was raised. Many people were healed and were set free from long standing issues, just from being in these Holy Ghost saturated meetings.

At the end of the services few people made an attempt to leave the building. They would sit in silence with eyes closed, soaking up the presence of God. Pastor Woodfield sometimes resorted to turning all the lights off and on in a light-hearted attempt to eject his congregation from the premises.

It was from this atmosphere I left to go to Bible College. From different departments of the church farewell parties were thrown for me. For several weeks before my departure I returned home from church to empty my pockets of ten and twenty pound notes in front of my amazed parents; gifts given from generous people who had quietly placed the money in my hand to help towards my future needs. I was showered with such love from the people of this church that it made it difficult for me to leave. Whenever I had previously left Birmingham I had always gone with a sense of excitement and anticipation. However this small church where God seemed to have taken up residence was where my heart had finally found a home, so it was with a sense of sadness that I departed even though I looked forward to the adventure I knew lay ahead.

Chapter 16

Study to show yourself approved

It was early in September, about five weeks after my twenty-seventh birthday that I stepped off the train at Dorking station, in Surrey. I carried my heavy cases through the exit barrier, and looking around intently. I hoped the fair-haired man I saw casually leaning against his car was the second year student that David Woodfield had arranged to meet me. As I began moving slowly towards him, he called my name. Relieved, I asked, "Are you Brian?" After assuring me that he was, he took my luggage from me to put into the boot of his car. Before taking me to the college, we drove to his flat where his wife was preparing lunch for us.

Brian and Jenny were members of the church in the North East of England that David Woodfield had pastored before he moved to Selly Oak in Birmingham. Both Brian and Jenny were in their mid thirties and had two children. Brian had been a policeman before coming to college. Soon after he became a Christian he felt he should go into the ministry. Jenny and the children had moved to a small flat in Capel village to be with him while he studied.

After lunch and a chat, I felt my anxiety rise when Brian said; "I had better take you over to the college." The grand, rambling building was well hidden from the busy main road by a profusion of trees, shrubs and a very large wall. I felt very grateful that Brian was there to steer me through the preliminaries. After I had said goodbye to him, I was led up a large sweeping staircase that reminded me of the 1940's film 'Gone with the wind.' I was then shown to a bedroom that would be my accommodation for the duration of my studies.

There was no one else in the room when I entered, but

judging from the clothes strewn across the beds and the mementoes on the bedside cabinets, it was evident the two beds in the bay window were already occupied. Of the remaining four beds, I decided to take the one opposite the door, because next to the bed was a small window. Through it I could see the tennis courts and a little of the countryside beyond, although I would have preferred a bed in the large bay window, from where the panoramic view across the gardens and the surrounding Surrey countryside was breathtaking.

Before I left home, as well as money, I was also given a lot of advice. The most beneficial, I thought, was to ask God to lead me to a good friend from among the students, which I subsequently did.

After I unpacked, I sat on my bed nervously listening to the sound of old and new students arriving in the corridor outside. Suddenly the door burst open and in bounded a pretty, dark haired girl. She wore jeans and a tee shirt, which made me feel a little overdressed for I had chosen to wear a dress on my first day. Against her milky white complexion it was hard to believe her thick, raven black hair had not been chemically produced, although I later discovered it was perfectly natural. Her parents, who were carrying much of her considerable possessions, including a record player and a collection of records, followed close behind. She introduced herself to me with a natural relaxed manner, telling me her name was Vicky Tufts, she was nineteen and this was her first day too. Of the vacant beds, the one in the corner farthest from the door and diagonal to mine was elected to be her home for the duration, chosen for the wall the bed was next to, a convenient place to house her bulkier belongings.

When her parents left, we chatted for a while. I discovered Vicky was from Luton, although she had hardly any trace of an accent. She was naturally friendly and I liked her immediately, not knowing this was the friend I had prayed for.

The other girls finally arrived. Sue Butler walked in and put her stuff on the bed next to mine. She was a confident, slender second year student from Guernsey. My first impression of her was that she was quite aloof, although I later changed my mind. She soon disappeared from the room to seek out friends she had not seen since the previous term.

The last to arrive was Chris, another second year student, from Stoke. Apart from her big, bush baby eyes, her appearance was fairly undistinguished. However she was very friendly for which, at that moment I was grateful, and willingly answered all the questions Vicky and I bombarded her with.

Chris told us the college was run by the use of a series of bells, which were rung throughout the day. These informed the students where they should be at that particular time. They began at 7am to wake the students. The last bell went at 10pm which was theoretically 'lights out'. I was amused by this information, and feared that it sounded more like the army or a convent than a college!

The girls who occupied the two beds in the bay window were language students from Iran and South America, Chris informed us. Apparently people from all over the world came to the college to study English. The language students shared accommodation with the theology students in order to use their English, therefore learn more quickly.

Even before I heard the bell, my hunger told me it was teatime. The recently returned Sue and Chris escorted Vicky and me down to the dining room. We queued along with the many other students in the recently built extension, which ran the full length of the rear of this elegant building. Vicky and I nervously clung together as we scoured the noisy dining room for a table with two seats together. When we were seated, I looked out at the fields beyond the college grounds through the large picture window. This certainly was a beautiful place, I concluded.

The first year students' classroom, we discovered the next day, was in the same enormous, converted sitting room the introductory meeting had been held in the previous evening. I tried to imagine the family that had once lived here and had sat around the huge fireplace, or had walked in and out of the French windows on the opposite side of the room leading into the large landscaped garden.

I had previously believed only the great and the good from Elim churches around the country would be gathered to study at the college. I had been afraid people would quickly realise I was neither. However, I discovered some people had travelled from across the world to be here. They also came from other denominations and all walks of life. Although some were intellectual and affluent types, others had come from appalling circumstances of deprivation. A melting pot of humanity the common denominator was that everyone had a great passion for Jesus. It was exciting to hear what had drawn each individual to this place.

A second year student told me that during the first term, as people got to know each other better, many initial friendships broke up, to be replaced by new ones. Nevertheless, the bond between Vicky and me only deepened as time went on, even though ours was an unlikely friendship. Vicky came from a middle class background and was much younger than me; she was also very studious having only recently finished Sixth Form College. Therefore she found no difficulty in researching for the essays we were instructed to complete. Her quiet, poised, dignified persona gave little indication of the mischievous sense of humour that lurked beneath.

I, on the other hand, experienced a complete culture shock when I arrived at the college. I could hardly understand what most of the lecturers were talking about; for me their theological terminology was like hearing a foreign language. Never before had I had to collect my own information to put into an essay, therefore I found it incredibly difficult. Fortunately, Vicky taught me how to study and to glean information from the countless books in the library.

We happily mingled with the other students, and other friendships soon grew. Someone else who became a good friend was Jackie Plumb. Although she was English, she had been brought up in Canada where her parents had emigrated when Jackie was a small child. They had moved back to England to manage a children's home in Cobham, Surrey. I listened fascinated, to her wistful tales of living on the edge of the Prairies, and about the children her parents had fostered; some were Native Indians. Her stories of going to school barefoot in summer, and having her father hose down the back yard in the winter to make a personal ice rink for his four daughters sounded like something straight out of Mark Twain's 'Tom Sawyer'.

Initially I pined desperately for the warmth of the people I had left at my home church. Fortunately when I returned at half term, I received such encouragement from the congregation I was spurred on with renewed enthusiasm. I decided that even if I cried every day for the two years I had planned to be here, I would not leave until I had completed the course; determined I would not disappoint the belief the congregation had in me.

The first Christmas I spent at Bible College was the most magical I had ever experienced. Everyone seemed to bubble over with the season's festive spirit. One cold, wintry night I joined a group of students who, accompanied by guitars and tambourines, went carol singing around the village. One or two of the more elegant residents invited the whole group into their homes for hot drinks and mince pies. However, it was equally delightful to sing outside the more humble dwellings and to see neighbouring bedroom windows thrown open, as neighbours leaned out to hear the music more clearly. Even though it would only be a few weeks before we saw each other again, an emotional farewell was said by everyone on the last day of term, when most students departed to spend the holidays with their families.

After the Christmas break I was much more settled and began to enjoy college life. A few bedrooms housed only two or three beds, but I was pleased that I was in a much larger room. The five girls I shared with all had a good rapport and there was often much giggling at bedtime. I loved to sit in my bed with my mug of hot chocolate as we relayed our experiences of the day to each other, to the background music from Vicky's record player.

During the second and third term, a number of casual friendships that began in the first term between male and female students blossomed into romance. There had been an immediate rapport between my friend Jackie and the young Scot Billy Williamson, who had come to college to train for the ministry. Their relationship grew very quickly and I was delighted to be invited to their wedding which was held at a little Anglican church near Jackie's home in Cobham, Surrey not far from the college. The reception was at the sprawling children's home her parents managed so, on a sunny day in August, the festivities were also enjoyed by the multitude of orphaned and abandoned children who were cared for by Mr and Mrs Plumb.

I arrived at Jackie's house a few days before the big day to help with the preparations. Although I shared greatly in Jackie's joy, I couldn't help wondering if the day would ever come when I would be preparing for my own wedding.

During the summer break Vicky and I visited each other several times. I had managed to buy an old rust bucket of a car, making it easier for me to drive up and down the motorway to her home in Luton, despite the ever present fear that it could break down at any time.

I had greatly looked forward to returning to college for the second year to see familiar faces again. Initially I missed the presence of the former second year students, some of whom had become good friends, but even without these; it was good to be back at college.

Jackie returned with Billy, but now she preferred to work in order to support her husband, rather than study. Despite often spending time together chatting over coffee, I missed her in the lectures. Nevertheless, it was not long before we all settled back into the routine.

Part of the curriculum was for students to minister at selected churches around the country. During my second year at college, together with nine other students, I went on a ministry trip to the picturesque, ancient city of York. After the two hundred mile journey, we finally arrived at our destination, tired and hungry. When we had eaten the meal prepared by members of the local church, we were told only three students would stay in York the others would be dispersed between two other churches in the region. Shortly after we had eaten, a young minister arrived to collect some of the students. Introducing himself he told us his name was John and he was from a church in Driffield, East Yorkshire. He seemed nice so when he called out the names on the piece of paper he was clutching, I was pleased one of them was mine. I was relieved that the other two names were guys I got on well with, ensuring this ministry trip would be an enjoyable one.

As we travelled to Driffield in John's car, we all enthusiastically told him our stories of how we became Christians. I gushed to him that I had been to Yorkshire before and how much I loved the county. Continuing my story I said, "It was through a conversation with a complete stranger while I was here several years ago, that my journey to becoming a believer began." When I saw he was listening intently, I asked him if he knew Dewsbury in West Yorkshire.

"I know it very well" he replied with a wry smile.

"Do you know Thornhill?" I continued.

"I used to teach at Thornhill School." He answered.

"Actually, I remember it was a teacher from Thornhill School that I had the conversation with."

John told me, "That could only be Christine, who was a colleague and once my wife's best friend. She came to our wedding, but we haven't seen her in ages. I'm sure we must still have her address somewhere if you would like it." I was utterly amazed, for I had long harboured a desire to tell Colin's old friend that through that single conversation I had sitting with her in her living room, I had eventually become a Christian. I had never made any attempt to find her, knowing it was impossible to do so. We lived in different parts of the country; I didn't even know her surname. I enthusiastically told John I would love her address.

Being in Yorkshire again was delightful, even though hearing the accent again caused great waves of nostalgia to sweep over me. I appreciated the warm welcome from everyone we met. Many showed their excitement, when I testified at the church that it had been through a visit to this beautiful part of the country, which had ultimately led to me becoming a Christian.

Having to say "goodbye" came round far too quickly. Nevertheless, with Christine's address in my luggage I looked forward to going back to college, eager to write to the teacher I had met only once. I wanted her to know that our chance meeting had totally changed the direction of my life. I was eager to tell her I was currently studying at Bible College, all because of that single conversation. I was overwhelmed with gratitude for although I had believed it totally impossible to find her; God had not only heard but miraculously answered the secret petitions of my heart. (Psalm 37:4)

When we returned to college I wrote my letter to Christine and posted it, with little expectation of a reply. However, surprisingly, only a week later I received a letter postmarked Dewsbury. Opening it, I found it was indeed from Christine. It read that she had only recently returned from working in

Africa with her new husband. Her letter read that she had been so encouraged by my letter she had read it out to the congregation at her church. She wanted me to go and stay with her because both she and the church members were eager to meet me. However, the streets of Dewsbury held too many painful reminders of the time I had spent with Colin. Although several years had passed, the memories of what I had lost were still very much alive, so with regret I felt I had to decline her very kind offer.

Going back to Yorkshire had caused a deep sense of loneliness to sweep over me. I felt tormented as I watched love blossom between couples at the college. Hope prevailed though when I read a book on prayer called 'The Fourth Dimension' by Paul Yonggi Cho which was to leave a deep and lasting impression on me. He told the reader not to pray vague prayers, but to dare to be very specific when requesting something from God. The book told the story of the time Dr Yonggi Cho first became a Christian, just after the Korean War that had ravaged his country. He had absolutely nothing so he asked God for a bicycle, a chair and a desk to help him pastor his meagre flock of Christians. When his prayer wasn't answered Yonggi Cho disappointedly asked God, "Why?" From his inner spirit he heard God say, "You haven't told me exactly what you wanted." Yonggi Cho then pictured the exact items in his mind. He boldly gave God the precise details of what he required, the kind of expensive timber he wanted the desk to be made from, the chair was to be a large swivel chair the kind an American *big shot* at the time would have and the bicycle was to have four gears. In these difficult times Yonggi Cho was asking for the impossible. Nevertheless he was asking from the God of the impossible and received everything he had asked for. This was a great lesson for him and his church grew to become the largest in the world.

Learning from his example, I told God exactly what I

wanted in my husband. The most important requisite on my list of requirements was that we share the same sense of humour. It was desperately important to me that we were able to laugh at the same things. Nevertheless, even as I prayed, as I had waited so long, I wondered if my husband was really out there or had I been mistaken when I believed God had promised me I would one day be married. I wanted to stop waiting for something that was never going to happen, therefore I asked God to give me a definite sign, one way or the other, and I would be satisfied.

A few weeks later when a group of students went to London in the college mini bus to hear a renowned preacher, I also decided to go along. The large auditorium soon became filled to capacity and a hush fell on the congregation when Arthur Wallis began to speak. The message he chose was called 'God's forgotten promises'. As his sermon progressed he asked the audience "Has God ever given you a promise that has not yet come to pass? Was it so long ago that you are now not sure whether God really spoke to you or whether you may have imagined it, but however much you try to get it out of your head you can't forget the promise." He continued, "That is because God did say it. He has not forgotten His promise to you. God always keeps His word." Those words could not have bore more deeply into my heart, had Jesus himself been standing on the platform speaking directly to me. Later that night, back in my room, I lay down to sleep with a mixture of elation and great peace, as my faith in God's promise was restored.

There was a great buzz of excitement amongst the second year students as the college year drew to a close, when many began to make specific plans for the future. Vicky decided to do a third year in order to study for a Degree. Although she pleaded with me to join her, I had neither the desire nor I believed the capability to do it.

Still pondering what I would do after college, while

cleaning the coffee bar one morning (my allotted task for the term), I suddenly had a very strong impression that I was to go back home to Birmingham. It was the last thing I wanted to do. It was only through the generous hospitality of Christian friends that I didn't have to remain at college during the previous Easter break, for my parents had forbidden me to return to their house during yet another argument. Now lamentably I believed God was telling me to return again.

The college was a hive of activity during the last week of term. Students cleaned every nook and cranny in preparation for the annual open day. The culmination of the week's activity was seeing the huge marquee erected in the grounds, in preparation for the students' graduation ceremony.

When the open day finally came, like everyone else, I was tired from the week's frenzied preparations. It was also very emotional, knowing this day was the finale we had worked toward for two years. Many casual visitors joined family and friends of the students, to look around the campus. I was moved to see Anne, Sue and several others from my church had come to support me on this momentous occasion. It was reassuring to know they were in the audience when I publicly received my diploma from the principal, Mr Gilpin.

Vicky had been in London for several days taking external exams, prior to the open day. It was not until I saw her hurriedly dash into the marquee, only minutes before it was her turn to collect her diploma, that I realised just how much I had missed her. I had learned so much from her gentle, selfless spirit that I had come to prize her friendship greatly. Although there was no doubt that we would stay friends, I knew this special time we had enjoyed together was coming to an end. The tears I had fought so hard to control all day began to overflow, and continued periodically throughout the remainder of the day.

When I first came to the college I had felt like a fraud, because I didn't feel I was worthy to be at this hallowed place.

It had not taken long to find that many other students felt the same way too. We were all just ordinary people whose once purposeless lives had been transformed by God. We had lived together for two years and had come to know each other so well, now most were going to ride off into the sunset to do something great for Jesus. I would not see many of them again this side of eternity. I would miss them so much. Seeing me wipe my eyes with a tear-sodden hanky, a male student from Belfast told me kindly in his lovely Irish brogue, "Sandie, this is what we came here for" which made me start wailing all over again.

A couple of days later, the dismantling of the marquee and clean up operation was complete, ready for the college to be closed for the summer. It was an enormous wrench to finally say a permanent goodbye to everyone. Some I had grown to love, a few had never progressed beyond being any more than mere acquaintances, but I was so sad to think I would never see them again.

My parents permitted me to move back into the family home, now that we were reconciled yet again. Although I looked exactly the same, going back home made me realise how much I had changed during the previous two years. Although the congregation at Selly Oak Elim church welcomed me with open arms and kindly applauded my achievements, they still believed I was the same dizzy blonde I had always been. However, I had been stretched so much through the experience, I knew I was different.

Chapter 17

Scotland calls again

During the last term of college Vicky and I, along with many other students, had attended the annually run Elim Conference. While there, I met a minister who had previously assisted David Woodfield in Selly Oak, while he studied at a nearby theological college. Over a cup of coffee, Graeme Parkin told me he had moved with his family to Scotland to pastor a church there. During the conversation he invited Vicky and me to consider working at a youth camp that was held annually at Dunkeld, a picturesque village in the heart of Scotland. Vicky and I delightedly agreed without hesitation.

Before I went to Bible College I would not have had the confidence to take on such a challenge. However, my two-year training taught me I was capable of much more than I had previously imagined.

The children aged from eleven to sixteen came from around the Glasgow area, as did most of the workers. It was good to return to Scotland, hearing the much loved, rugged Glaswegian accent again evoked poignant memories.

During the initial briefing, Vicky and I were informed we were to supervise a group of eleven-year-old girls. We were pleased, thinking this age group would be relatively easy to manage. Some of the girls were from deprived backgrounds with no church connection at all. The only reason they came to the camp was because it was the only way for them to have a holiday. Either Social Services or the church had paid for them to come. When the girls discovered their leaders were two unsuspecting English lassies, a small number gleefully thought this meant they would be able to cause as much havoc as they wanted to. We were both wrong.

The camp was held in the village secondary school. The boys were given the classrooms on the ground floor; the girls' dormitories were upstairs. Our group of girls were allocated the science lab as their dorm. Vicky and I didn't realise until we arrived on site that we would have to share the same sleeping quarters as the girls we were to supervise. The nine girls slept on camp beds down the other end of the room from Vicky and me. We slept near the door, just in case anyone decided to leave the dormitory during the night, to engage in mischief. No-one slept on the first night at the camp, all the children were so excited and determined to have fun at any cost, from the moment they arrived!

At first I wondered if Vicky and I might have taken on more than we could handle. A number of the girls were initially so contemptuous of us they would not co-operate with anything we asked of them. Vicky and I very rapidly learned to present a united front as the girls could be very persuasive in their attempts to avoid discipline! We discovered the best deterrent was to make the ringleader sleep down our end of the room, which they didn't like at all.

However, as the days went by we saw the barriers progressively come down as trust began to grow between us. Eventually Vicky and I would even go round at the end of every night to tuck each of them up in bed. Although they were rather embarrassed and objected at first, they later protested if one was missed out.

The change in many of the children at the camp was nothing short of miraculous. Some had appeared so hard when they first arrived, emotionally bruised by what life had already done to them. To witness the healing and transforming power of Jesus as He gently invaded their lives was an enormous privilege.

At the end of the fortnight, Vicky and I were both greatly humbled when we discovered the girls in our care had used some of their pocket money to secretly buy Vicky and me a goodbye gift. Although by the end we were both mentally and physically exhausted, neither of us would have missed the experience for the world.

Yet again I had to bid farewell to people I had grown to care about. It was particularly painful to say goodbye to Vicky. My heart ached, knowing that when the new term started she would be back at college, but I would not.

I could not believe that nothing more was to come out of my two years of training than to return home to do a secular job. I became quite exasperated when people asked me what I was going to do next because I didn't know myself.

I attempted to search for a job where I felt I might do some good. I travelled all the way up to Lancashire, where a bible college had advertised in a Christian magazine a clerical post with accommodation. However, I was aware the moment I arrived for the interview this was not for me. I realised I had wanted to be in the familiar environment of a bible college to recapture some of the security I had felt while studying at Capel.

I then applied for the post of resident House Parent at a Children's Home, even though I had had little rapport with the few children I had already come into contact with. Leaving the futile interview I realised this had been an even more ridiculous idea than the first one.

Dejected, I gave up the idea of trying to do something for God, and let my life settle back into the old familiar pattern I knew so well, that of living at home and working in a dead-end job.

Working in the offices of a sunroof-manufacturing firm for a short time, a new member of staff was recruited to work in the next office to me. I soon became good friends with Marilyn Hall, a thirty-two-year-old divorcee. Once or twice a week, after work, we would go to a nearby restaurant to eat and chatter until closing time, for circumstances had caused us both to be alone. When she told me she was shortly going on holiday to Israel, I cooed with envy. She said she had very little knowledge of the Bible lands but wished she knew more in preparation for her trip. So I invited her to a Bible study at my church and after attending for several weeks, my friend also became a believer.

At the dawn of 1978 I thought I could not be more miserable, but in fact by the end of the year I realised I could! The church leaders had started to buy the property that surrounded the church, with the intention of building a larger structure to accommodate the rapidly increasing congregation. In the interim, some of the properties were rented to students and a few needy members of the assembly. I was grateful for a room in one of these properties, for the tension at home had gradually escalated again. With regret I knew it was the last time I would reside under my parent's roof.

Like all the other houses in the rather run down area, the house I moved into was a typical gloomy Victorian terrace. Nevertheless, I loved being within walking distance of the church. The two other young women already sharing the house were Chris and Liz. Chris was a very likeable and attractive nurse. Having a boyfriend, understandably she spent most of her free time with him in her room. Hospitable Liz, being heavily involved with the church, entertained many people at our house. Each Sunday, she also hosted a Sunday school class in the sitting room, which was one of the reasons I found myself retreating more and more into the privacy of my own room.

I became increasingly depressed. I had mistakenly believed I would be married and have started my family by my thirtieth birthday; instead I was single and still living in bed-sit land. From my bedroom window I could see the dishevelled lonely old man in the bed-sitter across the road and believed I was looking into my own future. The voice in my head told me that living in shabby rented accommodation was always going to be my lot in life; it had been a long time since I had known such despair. I often felt I could not get through another day and wondered where God was. My current circumstances would have once led me to attempt suicide. However, now I knew that God was real I was afraid to take my own life, fearing what He would say when I met Him on the other side of the grave. Therefore, even though I could see no way out of my present plight, I was resisting that old urge and determined I would live my life until its natural end.

One winter's evening soon after the old year had merged into the new, I was casually browsing through the situations vacant column of the local evening newspaper, when I noticed an interesting vacancy advertised. It was in the Medical Records Department of the nearby sprawling Queen Elizabeth Hospital. With little expectation of a reply, because I lacked any previous experience, I half-heartedly applied for the post. However, later I received a letter inviting me for an interview. I could hardly believe my eyes when eventually I received a letter telling me I had been offered the post.

I started work around the middle of February and discovered I was able to take a very pleasant walk to work through the nearby Birmingham University grounds that separated my accommodation from the hospital. Working in the hospital environment was a fresh and exciting experience. My new colleagues could not have been more kind and helpful; going to work had finally become a pleasure.

Shortly however, I was to hear news that blighted my new found joy. I was devastated when Chris told me she was about to move out of the house, to live in a Council flat. It had been good to have her around, for we got on so well. Undeterred by my pleading she would not change her mind, instead she encouraged me to apply for a Council flat too.

I had never thought to ask the Council for a home before, so I was rather anxious even about the idea. There seemed such finality about it, a kind of confirmation that I would be on my own for ever. However, Chris was insistent and later told me the flat below hers was vacant, and urged me to apply quickly before it was offered to anyone else. As I pondered on this, from initially being filled with horror, I began to realise it was time to have a permanent home of my own. I became increasingly excited about the prospect, and mentally decorated every room. I decided my living room would be pink, because it was an unusual colour for a lounge at the time. I considered myself to be very innovative and different.

Never having had any real choice over previous accommodation, when the form asked where I wanted to move to I found the decision quite daunting. Fearful I may make a great error of judgement I asked God to direct me to where He wanted me to live. After living in so many gloomy bed-sitters, my only requirement for my new home was that it would be filled with light. I also prayed that God would give me some sign as evidence that, when I saw it, I was exactly where I was supposed to be.

The new flat that Chris had moved to was on the fourth floor of a nine-storey tower, not very far from my current accommodation. When she excitedly invited me to see it, I entered the flat to find several doors on either side of the lengthy hall. She opened each of them in turn to reveal two bedrooms, a bathroom, a separate lavatory and a cloakroom. Behind the door at the end of the corridor lay a spacious lounge. A large frosted glass partition separated the living area from the small kitchen. Light shone through the kitchen window filling the cosy living room with light. Opposite the kitchen was a glass door leading to a balcony from where a large pond could be seen just a short distance away. The numerous trees and shrubs surrounding it made the setting look quite rural. The pond was home to a family of ducks and a flock of Canada geese. Everything about her new home was idyllic. 'I could happily live here forever,' I thought, disappointed at having to go back to my gloomy lodgings.

I waited several months before I received information from the Council of a vacant flat to view. I was in the middle of final preparations to work at another youth camp, when a card fell through the letterbox, urging me to contact the Council immediately. When I did so, I was instructed to collect a key from their office, in order to look at a vacant property. I could hardly believe my ears when the person on the other end of the telephone told me the address, for it was the flat below Christine's. I was relieved to be told I could view the property when I returned from my imminent working holiday at the Elim Isle of Wight Youth Camp.

The children at this camp came mainly from churches and youth clubs in the South East region of England. I was relieved that I didn't have to share the accommodation with the children, but instead shared a tent with Liz who had joined me on this vacation. Getting a good night's sleep made the experience much less stressful than that of the previous camp. Although it wasn't quite as exciting as Dunkeld, it was still very rewarding.

When the holiday was over I travelled back to Birmingham on a mini-bus with some of the workers from the camp that like me were also without transport of their own. Excited, boisterous children, eager to get home to tell their parents about their adventures, were also travelling on the bus. During the journey, I became quite detached from all the noise generated by the lively children, as I closed my eyes and began to worship God. Suddenly a picture came into my mind. I saw a surgeon performing a delicate, life saving operation on a small child. Although a mask and surgical clothing hid his face, I could clearly see tears falling from his eyes. Somehow I knew the tears were because the child he was operating on was his own. I felt completely wrapped in a warm blanket of God's love, as in my spirit I heard the Lord say, "My child, I have been with you through all your pain. I have seen every tear you have wept and nothing you have been through has been in vain."

As soon as I returned home I went to see the property I had been offered. Anxiously turning the key in the front door of the flat, I wondered what condition it might be in. Apprehensively, I walked down the hall to the living room, knowing I was going to accept this property whatever its state because of its ideal location. As I opened the lounge door I gazed in awe at the wall in front of me, for it was covered in a beautifully patterned paper in a delicate shade of pink! I slowly looked around the room, my eyes feasting on everything I saw. Like Christine's flat above it was also filled with light. It was everything I had prayed for. I knew I had come home.

A great sense of peace fell upon me for I knew this was the Lord's doing. I knew the pink wallpaper was not only a sign that this was God's provision; but just like a rainbow, it was also a confirmation that He had not forgotten His promise to me. My hope that I would not always be alone turned to rock solid belief. I knew my husband was out there somewhere and in God's perfect timing we would meet.

Chapter 18

Wedding bells

I was not unduly concerned that I only had two items of furniture with which to furnish my new flat. One was a single bed I had bought in a sale and the other a pine chest of drawers purchased from a second-hand shop. I had acquired these items in an attempt to personalise my rather barren former bedroom. Fortunately, many church members came to my aid and individually supplied me with everything I needed for my new home. I was given a wardrobe for my bedroom, and lots of utensils for my kitchen. I was also the very grateful recipient of a pair of green curtains, a purple three-piece suite and a large yellow flowered carpet for my lounge. The fact that the multitude of colours clashed with each other, and also with the delicate pink wallpaper, was immaterial to me for each item had been given with love and I was overwhelmed with gratitude to the people for their bottomless reservoir of kindness.

Compared to earlier accommodation, living in my new flat was perfect luxury. I loved to be woken each morning by the sound of the ducks on the nearby pond. Each evening I would open the balcony door to listen to the local children playing in the neighbouring playground. Having just one floor between us, Christine and I saw each other nearly as often as we had when we lived together. The warm sense of belonging I felt at this latest abode made me feel quite settled; a heady new experience.

In contrast to the tranquillity of in my flat, the spiritual climate at church was gradually changing. Without realising it, I wonder if many in the congregation had begun taking for granted the amazing manifest presence of God in the meetings which seemed to have become familiar and commonplace. The extraordinary wave of God that had once enveloped the church began to recede. Only a few initially noticed the steady decline of liberty and freedom we had once enjoyed.

Some had not been particularly happy when the Holy Spirit had earlier come to disrupt the meetings, so they were not particularly disappointed when things eventually returned to 'normal'. However, there were others who grieved at the sense of the Spirit's withdrawal. We would never forget the precious days, when for a brief moment in time heaven came down and kissed the earth on which they stood, leaving their lives forever changed.

It was a considerable blow to many when one Sunday David Woodfield announced he was to leave the church. He was not only a charismatic leader but also an accomplished musician. Had we fully appreciated the uniqueness of his Spiritual gifts, they may have tried harder to make him stay. Sadly, it is often not until something is lost that its real value is recognised.

Another minister was quickly appointed to replace David. He was an excellent Bible teacher, although for me he seemed to lack the dynamism and the experience of his predecessor, being relatively new to the Ministry. The steadily declining situation at church coincided with improving changes taking place in my own life. As Christmas 1979 approached I was more content than I could ever remember being, but still alone, so I asked God if He would send me a special person to spend the holiday season with.

The festive season brought with it an invitation to a party in the home of a colleague at the hospital. Like the host, the majority of guests were also married. Not wanting to be on my own I asked Marlyn to accompany me, but being quite shy it was with great reluctance that she agreed to come. However, I was grateful that everyone from the office genuinely welcomed her, making my friend feel immediately at ease.

Val's tireless preparation throughout the day was duly rewarded with a very memorable Christmas party. Among the other single guests were Phil Peplow a former employee at the hospital and his friend Phil George, both in their early twenty's. Their reputation for being good fun had gone before them which for us promised an enjoyable evening.

The party was in full swing when the two Phil's eventually made a late appearance, but were every bit as entertaining as we had been led to believe they would be. Their large repertoire of anecdotes and funny stories had been perfected over a lifetime of friendship. We were told they had met as five-year-old children on their first day of school and had been friends ever since. Marilyn and I became the sole recipients of their humour as we laughed and danced with them throughout the night.

Phil Peplow was about five feet seven inches tall with a slim, wiry frame. Although only twenty-three, he conveyed an air of casual confidence that was very attractive and it soon became evident that there was chemistry between him and Marilyn.

Nevertheless, I was charmed by his much quieter friend's witty quips as we twirled around Val's living room floor. It was just two weeks before the party that Phil George had celebrated his twenty-fourth birthday. Although he possessed the same dry sense of humour as his friend, he was very different. Much fairer, stockier, and slightly taller than his friend he was obviously quite bashful, which I found rather endearing. I was immensely impressed that he was an auditor, for I had not previously moved in such illustrious circles with people who wore suits and carried briefcases to work. I thought it was very grand.

When eventually the party began to wind down in the small hours of the morning, and the guests drifted away, Marilyn and I were quite happy to accept a lift home from the two Phil's. We also agreed to accept the invitation to meet them the next evening, for the time spent in their company at the party had been magical. It had been a long time since I was in such enjoyable company; I wanted the delightfully giddy feeling to continue for as long as possible. Therefore when Marilyn phoned the next afternoon to inform me she had changed her mind that she didn't want to see them again I was crestfallen.

"Why ever not?" I implored.

"They're only kids," she said. "Don't you realise I am ten years older than Phil Peplow?"

I roared with laughter "Oh Mal, don't be so ridiculous!" I said, "We'll never see them again after today. Think of our date as a continuation of last night. It will be a nice way to round off the weekend and we'll try to avoid the subject of age, should it arise." To which she reluctantly agreed.

Phil George and Marilyn were already seated in Phil Peplow's car when I saw it pull up in front of my block of flats that evening. On this occasion they were not the scintillating company they had been the previous night. Having caught only a few hours sleep, by the end of the evening we were all so tired it was difficult to stay awake let alone make sparkling conversation. Nevertheless they still asked to see us the following Saturday.

Marilyn and I met the two Phil's several times over the Christmas period. We spent a very special New Year's Eve at Marilyn's little house, where she entertained us with her exceptional culinary skills. Although we continued to enjoy our evenings together, Phil George and I spent an increasing amount of time on our own, as did Phil Peplow and Marilyn.

I was reluctant to tell Phil that I was seven years older than him for fear it would herald the end of our growing friendship, although I was aware that I could not continue to put off the inevitable. I eventually told him while we chatted over a drink as we waited for the next showing of a film at a nearby cinema. By now my age had become a big secret between us so when I finally told him I was thirty-one my heart sank when he said quietly, "Oh." However, after thinking about it for a moment he joked, "You were nearly in the war!"

"I was not nearly in the war!" I retorted.

After a short silence I asked him if it made any difference.

"Of course not, you are still you, aren't you?"

However, I soon realised that telling him my age had made a difference, but not in the negative way I had expected. Because there were now no shadows between us our feelings only grew deeper.

At first I found his thoughtfulness and generosity rather confusing. One day as we were passing a lighting shop, I pointed out a lamp sitting in the window. I oohed and ahhed over the beauty of its brass stem and delicate handiwork of the glass shade, shaped to look like a budding flower. Several days later Phil presented me with a gift. I opened the packaging to find it was the lamp I had so admired. However, he was bewildered why I wept instead of the delighted response he had expected. Having only ever received presents for Christmas or my birthday I didn't understand why anyone would want to buy me such a gift for no special reason. There were other occasions like this and never having previously been lavished with such kindness I was initially rather suspicious of his intentions.

I had originally believed my relationship with Phil had been in answer to my prayer to have someone to share this one Christmas with, so I had expected our relationship to end with the Christmas period. When it didn't, I then thought the confession of my age would be the catalyst that would put an end to this very precious interlude in my life. By now I had lost my heart to this very gentle, humorous man, so I bravely asked God to end my relationship with Phil George for me if he wasn't the one God had chosen…but, God did not end it either.

It seemed like no time at all until winter burst forth into spring, which gave way to the summer when Marilyn and Phil were married. The ceremony took place on a warm July day in a little church close to her parents' home. Marilyn looked so very pretty as she walked down the aisle wearing a white Laura Ashley gown with a matching little scull cap towards Phil Peplow. The afternoon reception was held locally in a small hotel surrounded by picturesque gardens.

Most of the friends of the couple were those connected to the football team for which both Phil's played. After the meal and speeches were completed, I joined some of the wives and other girlfriends of the football players relaxing in the lounge of the hotel. We were all laughing and chatting merrily as Phil George walked past. Without stopping, he looked straight at me and said laughing, "I hope this doesn't give you any ideas!" I felt humiliated and outraged.

When Phil and Marilyn left to go on honeymoon, the party slowly dispersed. With other footballers and their spouses, Phil and I continued to celebrate at a nearby pub. However, he couldn't understand why I was so quiet. Every time he asked what was wrong I simply answered, "Nothing."

Later that evening, Phil and I went back to my flat for a cup of coffee. Again he implored me to tell him why I seemed so distant. I exploded with, "I would like you to know that I have no desire whatsoever to marry you. Don't think that I am waiting around for a marriage proposal from you, because I would not marry you if you were the last man in the world!"

So taken aback by what I had said he laughed in injured disbelief. After a few silent minutes he questioned quietly, "You would never marry me?"

"No, I would not." I snapped. My anger had begun to abate, when Phil asked again in a rather injured tone, "You really would not marry me?" By now my anger had completely drained away so I answered limply, "No." Silence hung thickly between us, eventually broken by Phil asking, "Will you marry me?"

"Ok." I giggled. We sat quietly for a few minutes, until Phil asked me when I thought we should get married. "There's no rush!" I answered, suddenly panicking at the enormity of our decision. The date we eventually decided upon was the thirtieth of May the following year, exactly two months before my thirty-third birthday.

Although he no longer pastored the church I wanted David Woodfield to officiate at the wedding. He still lived in the locality, so I went along to see him. Although Phil believed in God and had been happy to come to church he had never actually surrendered his life to Him. Deep down I knew that I could never marry anyone who did not really love God, so at my request David told me he would be happy to discuss the matter with Phil. A few days later Phil and I were seated on the settee in David's lounge. We discussed the wedding and also what the Bible says about marriage. At the end of our conversation David gave Phil a pamphlet entitled 'Steps to eternal life' about what it means to be a Christian.

The next night Phil told me he had read the leaflet David had given to him. He had even said the prayer at the end of the pamphlet that guided the reader as they invited Jesus to come into their life. "Although I have always believed in God," Phil told me, " I didn't realise that you could actually know Him." I was so delighted that I immediately phoned David Woodfield to tell him the news. He sounded as happy as I was, and added that it would give him the greatest pleasure to marry us.

Over the next few weeks Phil and I scanned the windows of major city centre jewellers, with the intention of cementing our decision with an engagement ring. Unfortunately the ones we liked were way out of our price range. I had almost given up hope of wearing an engagement ring. However, while we were out shopping locally one day, we came across a small, previously unnoticed jeweller. In the window were also displayed a small number of second-hand items. As we casually browsed, a particular ring caught my eye. A single diamond sitting on a band of white gold seemed to eclipse every other piece of jewellery in the window. Going inside to take a closer look, we were told the shop had only just purchased it. I loved the ring so much that it was unimportant to me that it had once adorned another's hand. The following week I could barely contain my joy as Phil slipped the beautiful diamond ring onto my finger as we celebrated at our favourite restaurant.

A few months later I was delighted when my old friend Vicky and her new young son Thomas, came to spend a few days with me. It was wonderful to see her again and for us to share face to face all that had happened since our Bible College days. She had eventually married the Irish student she began seeing during the third year of her studies and had since moved to Ireland. I was pleased to hear that the church in County Mayo where Vicky's husband John McAvoy was currently pastoring was doing so well.

Naturally, I could not resist the temptation to wave my new engagement ring at her. She told me she thought it was beautiful, but was not in the least surprised by what I had chosen. "You always said at college that you wanted a white gold, diamond solitaire ring when you got engaged."

"Did I really? I don't remember." I said, suddenly filled with awe. I marvelled at how God had led Phil and me to that little obscure jewellers shop, knowing the engagement ring I had once dreamed of owning was sitting in the window. God had not forgotten my desire, even though I had.

The following eight months were a whirlwind of activity as Phil and I prepared for our wedding. The ceremony took place at the little Elim Church we both now attended in Alton Road, Birmingham. Both David Woodfield and our current minister officiated at the proceedings. We chose the old hymn 'Great is thy faithfulness' because although I had doubted God many times He had remained faithful to me. I could not believe how nervous I was as I walked down the isle towards Phil and the fulfilment of the promise God had given to me all those years before. I wore a simple white wedding dress and was followed by two little bridesmaids, one Phil's seven-year-old niece the other Gail's three-year-old daughter.

Our small, intimate reception was held at my flat. Two members of the church, who were excellent cooks, organised the entire buffet as a wedding gift. They asked individual women from the congregation to make their signature dish, which they in turn gave as their own wedding gift. Phil and I and the wedding guests were staggered by the array of food on display which had been so lovingly given.

Chapter 19

Moving forward

Returning from our honeymoon we continued to live happily in my much loved flat by the duck pond. During this contented period in my personal life, our kind young pastor finally seemed to bow to the realisation that he was not equipped to revive the decline our church was going through, so he decided to leave and returned home, a sadder but wiser man. His replacement could not have been more different. He was a mature family man, much more experienced and confident. However his determination to take control and stamp out what must have seemed to him excesses in the meetings severely hampered any remaining evidence of the move of the Holy Spirit. Many were content with the status quo, happy in the knowledge that nothing unusual was going to take place when they came to church. Others felt frustrated with the uninspired worship and longed for the days of yesteryear when it appeared that the Holy Spirit moved at will.

The gulf between the two differing opinions widened to such an extent that a meeting was arranged for all the members to air their views on the current situation. As nothing was resolved at this meeting as weeks went by numbers attending the church dwindled greatly.

Phil and I also eventually felt my once cherished haven no longer held anything for us so we prayed that God would somehow lead us to another Spiritual refuge. A number of weeks had passed when we received a phone call from a friend and previous member of the church inviting us to join a small gathering of people who were also former members of our church but had not yet located anywhere else to worship.

The meeting took place in our friends' home the next Sunday morning, taking the form of a church service. It was so refreshing to be with people I held very dear again. One of those present, Bill, had once been a deacon in the church, but now sadly, was also without a Spiritual home. He invited the people present to a further meeting at his own home the following week. It was fortunate that he owned a large house, for word had been passed around and so many exiles from our former church arrived to this open invitation that they not only filled the large elegant conservatory, but also overflowed into the kitchen and dining room. While we were there Bill called David Woodfield, who was living in America, to discuss the situation because we all felt at a loss of what to do next and Dave had not only been our Pastor but a friend to us all.

The next thing we heard was that he had come over to England to personally talk to us because we all still thought of him as our Pastor! It was wonderful to see him walk in to a later meeting. We enjoyed a great time of prayer, worship, and singing. So many people turned up that David's pastor's heart was moved with compassion for this bereft shepherd-less flock of people. To his friend Bill, whose house we were at, he later volunteered to lead this congregation should an appropriate building be found.

Two women who had been at this meeting took up the challenge to find somewhere to worship. They located a nearby hall and asked the caretaker if they could hire it every Sunday morning for an indefinite period of time. They were jubilant to hear the answer was a resounding "Yes!". The building and location could not have been more perfect. Although it was in the leafy grounds of a local college, the front of the building was close to the main road and near to a bus stop, convenient for those without transport of their own. The building itself had all the necessary amenities; a stage, a kitchen, and although the seating was fairly minimal, the auditorium could be opened up to seat between five or six hundred people when required. David was true to his word and returned with his family from America to pastor the church. In September 1982 the Christian Life Centre was born.

*****

Phil and I were to enjoy worshiping there for many years to come. With David Woodfield at the helm the church grew steadily. From time to time it even became necessary to open up the auditorium to accommodate the increased congregation. However, although the Holy Spirit was given free reign, we were never again to see the amazing outpouring we had briefly enjoyed in those former days at Alton Road.

When Phil and I eventually decided to start a family we began to save in earnest. I didn't really want to bring up children in a third floor flat, so the money we saved was for the deposit on a house for our future family. However we were only able to save a small amount each month for there was not much money left over after we had paid our bills. We decided it would probably take years to accumulate the amount of money we needed.

Nevertheless I was not perturbed, for I decided to ask Jesus for a house instead. I gave a lot of thought about what would be important to me in my ideal home. My perfect house would be a three-bedroomed semi-detached. As I had inherited a love of flowers from my father, I would like my lounge to be at the rear of the property, with a door leading directly into the garden. I imagined myself in the summer months gazing out through the open door into my flower filled sanctuary. A dining room was also important to me because Phil and I both enjoyed cooking for our friends. I could see us all eating around a big table in our new home. I prayed for a small kitchen so that everything would be at hand, but a large hall to welcome in our many guests.

Phil was mildly amused that I dared to believe Jesus would grant so large and explicit a request. But I questioned him, "Doesn't the Bible say in Matthew 7:11 "If you then, being evil know how to give good gifts to your children, how much more will your Father who is in heaven give good things to those who ask Him?" I didn't know when I would receive it, but having learned to wait on God I was quite confident that one day we would live in the house I had prayed for. Had I not already seen God do amazing things in answer to prayer?

In the meantime Phil and I decided to go ahead and start a family. I was a shade disappointed that I became pregnant immediately because it meant the baby would be born in February, already overcrowded with family birthdays. I had wanted our baby to be born in the spring when the flowers were in bud and the sun was beginning to get warmer.

Now that we had grown up I enjoyed a much better relationship with my younger brother Bryn. He was now in his twenties, married with a new baby daughter who had also been born the previous February. He and his wife Kay had recently moved to a delightful detached house, having waited patiently for several years in their Council flat to be re-housed either by the Council or a little known private housing association they had found, which had been the vehicle for them getting their new house.

I was enjoying a pleasant sunny afternoon in his garden, when I wistfully told my brother how I envied him his house and especially of having a garden. Bryn had also inherited our father's love of gardening, and was in the process of making his beautiful. He quickly disappeared into the house and came back with the address of the housing association. Although I was thankful to him, neither of us really had much hope of any success in sending an application to them. The company had once been a thriving concern and owned nearly all of the houses in the area. Now it was greatly depleted having sold off most the properties over the years when tenants had either vacated or died.

Nevertheless later in the week Phil and I completed and returned the application form we had received from the company, without giving the matter further thought. Several months later, and heavily pregnant, while at work I received a telephone call from my husband. Very excitedly, he told me he had just received a telephone call from the housing association, telling him a property had become available for us to view. Although I was delighted that we might be getting a house I felt uneasy about it. I knew from the description the house was the same as the one I had grown up in, totally different from what I had prayed for. The location was terribly inconvenient too, a great distance from the main bus route to our church. Should anything go wrong with our car I envisaged difficulty in getting there. On the other hand, if we passed up this opportunity we might wait for years before another house became vacant. I felt very ungrateful and confused as I wondered what we should do. Nevertheless we decided to take a look at the property later that evening when Phil came home from work.

Driving toward the house that dark November evening, my husband told me he had a surprise for me, "After I phoned you today the woman at the housing association rang back." He said, "She told me another house is about to become available which she thought might be more suitable for us. That's where we're going to now." Phil told me the house was in Josiah Road, Northfield. Having grown up just around the corner I knew the pretty tree lined road well. The houses were much larger than the one I grew up in. Maybe that was why people in the area once considered it to be the 'posh' road.

Eventually the car came to a halt outside the house. As expected it was in darkness. We couldn't go inside for we didn't have the keys yet. Nevertheless when we got out of the car to take a closer look, Phil excitedly asked me what I thought of it. I smiled back at him in silence for I was not able to answer; it was as much as I could do to fight back the tears of joy, for I knew without even looking around this beautiful property it was the house I had prayed for.

Within weeks we had moved into our new house. There were two reception rooms. Naturally, Phil and I chose the room at the rear of the building for the lounge which had a French window leading out into the garden. The previous tenant must have been a keen gardener for in the spring we discovered beautiful flowers springing up everywhere. The kitchen was small and the hall was large, just as I had asked for and we eventually entertained many guests in the large dining room at the front of the house.

We had been living in the house just over a year when I received a phone call from the housing association telling me the company was selling some of their properties. We were asked if we would like to buy the house we lived in, as we were sitting tenants the cost would be greatly reduced. Needless to say we agreed, so within two years from the time I began to pray, we were buying the house I had dreamed of.

The place was still in a state of disarray when on the eighteenth of February, four months after we had moved in, our beautiful daughter Lindsay was born. I had been told a mother's love is the most overpowering feeling in the world. Even so, I was still surprised by the torrent of emotion this little five pounds nine ounce bundle of humanity evoked in me.

As she grew I loved to watch the interaction between her and her devoted father. If she hurt herself in any way it was to him she would run for comfort. He would sweep her up into his arms while making ambulance noises. Then placing her onto the settee he would say, "Show doctor daddy where it hurts." The place would receive either a kiss or a tickle, followed by squeals of laughter from our delighted child.

It was not until some time after Lindsay's third birthday

that I realised it had been quite a while since I had thought about the baby that had been aborted, once never far from my mind. Each February I wondered on which day he or she would have been born, for even this baby would have had its birthday in February. Every year that passed I knew what age he or she would be, I could not forget; for it is far easier to remove an unborn baby from a woman's body than it is to take it from her mind. Nevertheless, I thanked God that February had become a month for celebration replacing the sadness and regret. Indeed "He had turned my mourning into dancing." Psalm 30:11

Chapter 20

When the cloud moves

Following a five-year break to look after our daughter, I returned to work when Lindsay started school. For a few hours each day I filed correspondence into patients' medical notes at a local GPs surgery which suited me perfectly. I worked there for many years for the witty banter exchanged between members of the clerical staff could be very entertaining and my restless spirit was no more.

I was experiencing a very content period in my life; little did I know however that quite soon change was going to take place. After ministering at the church for over nine years, David Woodfield decided it was time to resign from his post to go on to pastures new. At David's final service the men in leadership had nothing but praise for him. They complimented David on how the church had expanded during his ministry, even awarding him a generous gift to show their gratitude. Although it appeared that nearly everyone seemed happy with the situation, I didn't understand why I felt such overwhelming grief.

I was greatly relieved that the services continued to be just as lively as they had been before David departed. The church leaders were hopeful they would be able to recruit someone equal to David Woodfield's calibre, and hopefully see again a mighty move of the Spirit of God.

Although the pastor that replaced David Woodfield was a gentle, kind, man, he possessed few of David's exceptional talents. Sadly again I felt the meetings were becoming progressively more laboured and sterile and I despondently watched again many leave the church.

The feelings of dissatisfaction I felt continued to ebb and

flow for a long time. They subsided a little when I gave a lift home to a member of the congregation following a mid week meeting. Mandy Scott had attended the church since childhood for her parents had been members as far back as "Alton Road days". Mandy had only recently returned from teaching in the Philippines, although I had previously been aware of her in the church we had had little reason for contact. She was now in her early twenties and I was the busy mother of a small child. Although there was an almost twenty year age difference we seemed to connect immediately as we sat chatting outside her house.

Mandy told me she too felt the same inexplicable yearning that I felt, so we agreed to pray together once a week to see what happened. We became good friends and continued to meet each week for many years for we saw amazing answers to prayer, seeing at first hand the truth of the scripture in Matthew 18:19, "If two agree on earth concerning anything they ask, it will be done for them by My Father in heaven."

When the Christian Life Centre celebrated its tenth anniversary, a renowned local pastor was invited to preach. David Carr had been a friend of the church since the days at Alton Road when he had been a member of the congregation. David ended his message by inviting the young people to hear an American called Rick Godwin preach at his church.

A couple of weeks later, arriving at my house to pray Mandy enthusiastically informed me that a number of the youth from our church had decided to go to David Carr's to hear the preacher he had spoken about.

"Do you fancy going?" I asked

"Oh yes." She answered.

Without hesitation I put on my coat and prepared to drive the twelve-mile journey, leaving my daughter in the capable care of her father.

When we arrived we found the large church was already

nearly full but Mandy and I soon found seats near the back of the large auditorium. I was quite pleased with where we were seated, for we were able to make a quick exit at the end of the meeting before many others had a chance to move. The worship was simple but very refreshing and Rick Godwin's preaching every bit as dynamic as we had been told it would be. Being here was wonderful for the atmosphere seemed charged with the presence of God. Something inside me stirred as I now understood the restlessness and hunger I had felt for a long time was to sense again the closeness of God with whom I had once been so familiar. I couldn't wait to get home to tell Phil all that I had experienced in the meeting.

Therefore we were both in the congregation the next time Rick Godwin returned to the Renewal Christian Centre. He talked about the blessings of obedience and spoke about the Children of Israel wandering in the wilderness. During his sermon he made an almost off the cuff remark that pierced my heart like an arrow. It was simply 'when the cloud moves, you move with the cloud' referring to the Israelites moving from one camp to another when God told them to. In that random comment I knew God was telling me the time had finally come for me to leave the Christian Life Centre.

I was very reflective on the journey home. I had toyed with the idea of leaving my church for a long time; I was now quite sure it was the right thing to do. My husband was perfectly content where he was so I knew it would be God's doing if he accompanied me on the day I knew I would finally leave the church.

In the days that followed I felt greatly burdened as I pondered on what I believed God had said to me for I not only had to tell my husband of my intentions, but also the congregation at my church who had been so kind to me.

A short time later, Phil attended a Men's conference at the church David Carr pastored. The last meeting was on a Sunday morning but recovering from flu, sadly I was unable to attend. Nevertheless, when Phil and some friends who had also attended, returned home, they all piled into my house eager to tell me about the great time they'd had. There was a wonderful jovial atmosphere as each eagerly recounted what they had enjoyed most about the service. When Phil and I finally waved goodbye to the last visitor I felt so exhilarated by all the chatter it was almost as if I had been there myself.

I felt the service was more dead than ever at my own church the following Sunday. I knew it was time to leave even though I had no idea what I was going to do next. It did not take long for members of the congregation to hear what I was planning and many expressed their reservations of the wisdom of my decision. The next few weeks leading up to my final departure were harrowing for I loved these people who had loved and supported me so much over the years. Now believing I really must have heard from God for I was so unshakable, I was greatly relieved when Phil agreed to go with me, where ever that may be.

After some discussion the church we decided to attend was the Renewal Christian Centre that was pastored by David Carr. To move to this much larger church where we knew so few people was a strange experience and I was very glad my husband was at my side when we arrived for our first service for I was very nervous. It gave me some insight into how a refugee must feel knowing they would never again return to their old country, for I knew I had burned my bridges.

Happily though, our daughter Lindsay joined the Sunday school and very soon had an abundance of new friends. Phil also made friends very quickly due to attending the men's ministry. It was a great relief to find my anxieties about the move had been unfounded and within a short time our new church felt like home to the whole family.

Phil and I happily became increasingly involved with the work at the Renewal Christian Centre. Eventually we were asked to be part of a newly formed team of advisors that would assist new people in their pursuit to know more about the Christian faith. A Christian counselling course was set up to help equip the virgin 'counsellors' in their new role. The intense course lasted for three terms and covered subjects as diverse as divorce, drug and alcohol abuse, bereavement, and post-traumatic stress disorder. Although it was hard work, the course was very helpful, even though there were subjects some students found difficult to deal with because they echoed situations from their own lives.

When a guest speaker from a Pregnancy Advice Centre came to talk about abortion, I did not suspect how traumatic it would be for me. The woman talked quite openly about the devastation her abortion had caused to her marriage and to her mental health. It was the first time I had heard anyone discuss her personal experience. Furtively, I glanced around the room at the fifteen or so men and women casually taking notes and wondered if anyone noticed my acute discomfort, for I felt totally exposed, believing my guilt and shame must somehow be evident for all to see. I could hardly breathe or concentrate from the pounding in my ears as my heart beat so fast. When the class was over I hastened to the exit for some much needed fresh air.

Later that week I told my friend Mandy what had happened at the training session, having previously confided to her about my abortion and the circumstances surrounding it. I told her I thought my own experience might help others, and that I would like to counsel women in similar situations. She reminded me that she was a volunteer counsellor at a local Pregnancy Advice Centre. I was delighted to hear there was a vacancy at the centre.

Following a brief interview with the manager, I registered for the next available training session, which was to last just a few weeks. Many of the women on the programme had also had abortions. It was beneficial to see how, like me, some had previously been too ashamed to speak about it openly;

therefore as the sometimes harrowing course progressed, much emotional healing took place for many of the women who attended.

Eventually the day came when I nervously took my place at the local branch of the National Pregnancy Advisory Centre, alongside my friend Mandy. Located on a busy main road it was open for just one morning a week. The women who called in were from all walks of life, and their reasons for attending the clinic were just as varied. Although many came simply for the free pregnancy test given on request, others required a confidential chat with someone outside their circle of friends. The occasions we saw a positive input to a person's life were worth the sometimes mundane or quiet periods when few came to the centre.

The day an older mother visited the centre, expecting her fourth child, was very exciting. Her husband faced possible redundancy and with another baby on the way she was quite anxious about the future. The delivery of her unplanned third child had been very difficult, causing great anxiety about the birth of the baby she was carrying. Because of her current circumstances, family and friends advised her to terminate the pregnancy. This pleasant lady came to us seeking an independent and unbiased listening ear. After a long discussion over a cup of tea, my colleague asked finally, "If the circumstances were perfect would you still opt for a termination?"

"Oh no, I wouldn't." She answered without hesitation.

Her eyes lit up as she realised she had answered her own question. My colleague and I prayed that her next delivery would be much easier than the previous one had been. Before she left we gave our client a pair of bootees as a gift. Showing them to her two-year-old son she told him, "They are for the new baby!"

Turning to us she said, "That's the first time I've called it a baby." Later that evening it felt very rewarding to tell my husband, "Today I helped to save someone's life."

When a girl around sixteen or seventeen years of age came in for a pregnancy test, in an attempt to make light conversation, my colleague asked her if she had a boyfriend. "No." she answered sheepishly. She then told us falteringly that she had been raped while waiting alone for a bus to take her home after a night out with her friends in the centre of Birmingham. Hanging her head in shame, she told us a youth had grabbed her, took her up an ally and forced himself upon her. We were the first people she had disclosed this information to.

Memories came flooding back, as I saw how degraded this young girl clearly felt. Instinctively I fled from my chair and knelt in front of her. With my forefinger, I lifted her chin until her eyes met mine. "Don't you dare hang your head in shame," I told this frightened little girl "You did nothing wrong. It wasn't your fault. Do you understand?" She answered by nodding her head. I then told her God considers what had been done to her so heinous that in Bible days that man would have been hunted down and executed for what he did. I then sat on the arm of her chair and cradled her head in my arms. As I stroked her hair, I prayed that God would release her from the shame and self-reproach I knew often tormented the victims of this kind of crime. We were all very relieved when the pregnancy test came back negative. She left the centre with a genuine smile in her eyes.

Chapter 21

Hearing from heaven

Life continued on fairly uneventfully for some time until one Sunday morning when, as would sometimes happen, Niall Cluley, a member of the congregation, and an excellent Bible teacher preached the sermon. This week his message was entitled 'Walking out of curses into blessings.' He described how negative words said to a child can imprison that person throughout their whole life. Deep wounds inflicted by the careless spiteful words of a parent, teacher or even other children can severely hamper a person's life, he told us. Niall continued by saying the Blessing of God on a person's life nullifies any curse put on them by the malicious words from another's mouth.

I suddenly realised my father's words of contempt, repeatedly said to me throughout my childhood and youth had cast a long shadow over my life. I had unwittingly carried the belief that I was useless and of little consequence, for I had continued to believe the words of my father rather than what the Bible said about me. Since becoming a believer I made every effort to hide the person I thought I was. As Niall continued to preach I received a revelation of the entirely new and whole person I had become the very day I surrendered my life to Jesus.

Some time later Pastor David Carr, who had grown from the fiery young evangelist I had once known to an eloquent internationally recognised speaker, prophesied over me. Among the things he told me was that God had not yet revealed to me why I had gone to Bible College. When I first returned home at the completion of my studies I had been extremely disappointed that I did nothing more exciting than to go back into secular employment. Initially, I felt studying theology for two years had been a waste of time, unlike some other students who had gone onto illustrious careers. However, over the years I came to realise what a great privilege it had been for me to have had the opportunity to study the bible in such great depth in the heart of the beautiful Surrey countryside. Some of the people I had met there I would never forget. It had been over twenty years since I had attended, so I thought it was unlikely my earlier training would be of much value now. Nevertheless there had been times when alone in the secret place with God I had cried out to be used in a greater measure. I had not seen it materialise but I didn't mind because I was now happily married and watching our daughter grow was an indescribable delight. Nevertheless, there were still times when that smouldering desire to do something more for God than I was currently doing would sometimes flicker, although I couldn't imagine what more I could do.

One Tuesday evening, I attended the weekly prayer meeting at Renewal Christian Centre as usual. It was not a rare practice for David Carr to call a person out from the congregation, in order to tell them something that God had told him of their future. "Prophecy" is mentioned in the Bible as a gift from God to encourage and comfort people unlike the counterfeit gift of fortune telling I had once hankered after as a teenager that always seemed to lead to sorrow. This particular evening I was shocked to hear my name being called. When I saw people turn round to look at me I realised I hadn't imagined what I had heard, so I nervously left my seat to walk to the front of the church. Standing in front of the congregation, David told me, "You have carried a burden for many years, in February it will be lifted." He then prayed for me before I returned to my seat. Although I couldn't think of anything I was particularly worried about, I looked forward with interest to whatever would unfold.

By the time February came round I had almost forgotten the words spoken over me on that cold December evening. However, one dismal February afternoon I was watching The Oprah Winfrey Show on television. The knowledge I gained from the inspiring teaching from her current crop of guest counsellors was a great asset both to me and when I had occasion to counsel others at church.

Oprah's guest this day was John Gray, the author of the best selling book 'Men are from Mars Women are from Venus.' He discussed the reasons why certain random comments can trigger inexplicable and irrational behaviour. When the audience were invited to ask questions, a very elegant, young, olive skinned woman wanted to know why an occasional casual disparaging remark from her husband aroused such instant anger in her, to the point that she almost wanted to kill him. That this petite, refined young lady could entertain such savage emotions caused a ripple of laughter around the studio. John Gray invited this professional musician onto the platform for further discussion. He asked her to remember back to her childhood relationship with her overbearing father. He also asked her to try to remember the first time she felt this rage. It transpired that when her husband occasionally spoke to her in a demeaning way it subconsciously took her back to her childhood, reminding her of the way her father had often verbally belittled her causing fury to be instantly unleashed when her husband did the same thing. Her smile grew as she knew she was free having now made the connection.

As I listened to this woman talk about her childhood, I was mentally transported back to my own. I could not remember ever having a proper conversation with my own father. Although he was by no means cruel, our communication was mostly through the usual pleasantries, "hello", "goodbye", "goodnight", or when he chastised me for something I had done wrong. Somewhere in my child's mind had grown the belief that I was invisible. As an adult that belief was still buried in my subconscious. The feelings of ineptitude that had plagued me from childhood I could now see were linked to past experiences; they were not part of my personality at all, as I had previously believed. In the days that followed, armed with this new knowledge, I noticed I was no longer filled with anxiety when around the professional people I came into daily contact with. To feel equal to anyone I conversed with was an unexpected and delightfully novel experience. "When you know the truth, the truth will make you free." John 8:32.

I was so excited that what God had told me through David Carr had come true exactly as and when he said it would that I could not wait to get to the next meeting at church to tell him. The following Tuesday I purposely got there earlier than usual to share my news with him as he waited for people to arrive for the prayer meeting. I was happy to comply when he asked me to tell the congregation what had happened. When I later finished relaying my story to them, David prophesied over me yet again. This time he told me that during the first week of June of that year I would receive so much wisdom and knowledge I would wonder where it all came from. He told me that as I read the Bible it would speak to me as never before. Also my faith was going to become mature in a way I had not previously known. He finished the prophecy by adding almost as an after thought, "This is the year you will know why you went to Bible College." I pondered on all that had been said and waited expectantly to see what would happen.

On the very first Sunday in the month of June, waiting for me when I got home from church was a message on the telephone answer machine from my sister Gail; it was about our mother. My parents had moved house and now lived in a small retirement apartment in the same small rural village that my sister lived. The message told me that our mother was in the Intensive Care Unit at the local Queen Elizabeth Hospital in Birmingham, a sprawling, teaching unit that dealt primarily with serious illnesses. Anxiously I phoned my father to find out why she was there. He tearfully told me that while watching the television the previous evening my mother suddenly was unable to control her head and neck movements. She continued to lose control over the rest of her body until by the time the ambulance arrived she was paralysed from head to foot. My father gave me strict instructions not to pass this information on to my brother, who my parents had not spoken to for several years, although no one could remember the origin of the initial disagreement.

Immediately, Phil drove me to the hospital where to my horror, I found my mother unconscious and connected to a multitude of machines. We were told these machines were keeping her alive until the doctors could discover what had disabled every part of her body.

After a series of tests the medical staff diagnosed Guillan-Barrie syndrome, a very rare virus that can attack anyone of any age, particularly those whose bodies may have been weakened by a bout of influenza or even just a common cold. At the time it wasn't certain if she would recover from this very close brush with death. We were told the recovery period from this very debilitating illness can be up to two years.

After I had finished work at lunch time the following day I rushed to the hospital to visit my mother and was delighted to find her conscious; but she looked so frail that I wanted to weep. Although she had lost the power to speak, it gave me hope to see that she recognised me.

At the counselling classes I was still attending we had been taught that a dying person's wishes were to be respected above anyone else's. So despite my father's firm instructions to the contrary, I asked my mother if she wished to see my brother. With obvious great effort she answered the question by a slight nod of her head. To make sure I was correct in understanding what she wanted, I asked the question a different way. "Dad said you are not to see Bryn. Do you agree?" She managed to slowly turn her head from left to right, as a tear trickled down her cheek. "I will go and get him for you." I said, as I kissed her goodbye.

I left the hospital to drive to the workshop where my brother was employed as a tyre and exhaust fitter. As I walked toward him, seeing my distress, he affectionately put his arms around me and asked me what was wrong. I sobbed to him what had happened to our mother. "She wants to see you." I wept, and without any hesitation he said, "Let me wash up and I'll come."

Being the youngest child and a boy, my brother had undeniably been the apple of our parents' eye right up until his marriage at the tender age of twenty. My parents seemed to find it difficult to come to terms with another person residing in first place of his affections. Continual antagonism toward him and his wife progressively destroyed their once fond relationship. Therefore we both knew it was more duty than desire that led my brother to the hospital that day. Nevertheless, to see my brother weep so bitterly at the pitiful sight of our mother clinging to life by a thread tore my heart to shreds. I knew he partly wept for the wasted years lost in hostility. It could have been so different. However we were both pleased he had been to see her, for neither knew if this might be the last opportunity.

I was not looking forward to the telephone call I would later make to my father, anticipating the row that would inevitably follow when I told him I had taken my brother to the hospital. However, I was surprised and relieved to find he was already aware that Bryn had been to see her, for my mother had managed to convey it to him during his visit later that day. In fact, my father told me, he was glad I had taken my brother to see her. However I was horrified to hear him venomously snarl, "It's you I don't want there!" I listened in absolute horror as I heard him spew insults at me down the telephone. It seemed angry feelings my father had once felt toward me when I was a rebellious teenager still rancoured with him.

I felt swept away in a torrent of emotion as old wounds of rejection were reopened. I heard with dismay that my brother who had been shunned by my parents for over six years was more desired at my mother's hospital bedside than me. Tears dropped from my chin as I falteringly asked, "Dad, what did I ever do to make you hate me so much?" It seemed he had difficulty finding the answer, "You just don't care!" he said eventually. My head swam with his unbelievably inaccurate words ringing in my ears, as I gently replaced the receiver.

As dawn was breaking the next morning, the taste of salty tears was still in my mouth as I woke from my night of fitful sleep. The strong arms of the man I loved pulled me closer when he realised I was awake. "Why does he hate me so much?" I sobbed, still reeling from the previous evening's conversation. "I love you," my husband whispered tenderly, as he kissed away my tears.

I cried out to God in desperation like I never had before for I needed to know where all this anger and hatred had come from. Just as David Carr had said earlier in the year, God not only heard my cry but also answered as I received unprecedented revelation into the history of my family.

That day I drove along my usual route to work. As I absent-mindedly thought about my family and recent events, I remembered how envious I had once been of the relationship my sister Gail enjoyed with our father. It appeared, with such little effort she could persuade him to do anything she wanted. Gail's often theatrical attempts to beguile him into letting her have her way always greatly amused him. Unexpectedly I suddenly understood that there was a *controlling spirit* at work. I had not only had personal experience of "spiritual activity" but the Bible explains that there is a realm other than the natural one that we see with our physical eyes so the revelation of demonic influence in the family did not come as a shock!

However, I was surprised that it wasn't Gail who controlled my father, but the reverse. I could also see quite clearly that my relationship with my father had been so volatile because that controlling spirit had vehemently hated my father having such little power over his wayward and wilful eldest teenage daughter.

While I pondered over the thoughts that had come to my mind, a memory from my childhood came back to me. As I wondered where this controlling spirit might have come from I remembered my father telling me his mother had been able to tell fortunes. I am aware that often unwittingly, by the presence of a demonic spirit there are people who genuinely can look into people's future, although there are many charlatans who practice the art.

When the current situation with my father later eased, I asked him if my grandmother had ever told fortunes. "Oh yes. She was very good!" he boasted proudly. "She was happy to tell anyone's fortune until she told a client a relative would soon die. When the woman's brother died in an accident within weeks of the reading, my mother never picked up the cards again." 'So there was an evil spirit abroad in the family,' I thought.

As I thought about my childhood, different scenes from the past moved graphically across my mind. One particular memory was seeing my father proudly lead his mother around his cherished garden, waiting in eager anticipation for her to compliment his achievements and how crestfallen he had been when only derision came forth. Even when he was an adult I realised my father had still craved praise from his mother.

Sadly he was as oblivious to his own children's need of their father's approval as his mother had been to his. Memories returned of past attempts I had made to win my father's applause, which also invariably failed. It dawned on me that my father had been quite unable to demonstrate the love I had desperately sought from him because he too was subconsciously bound through his own childhood experiences. This revelation was remarkably freeing.

At one of my counselling classes around that time the subject discussed was of different aspects of child abuse and how it can continue to affect a person's adult life without them even realising the cause. It had never previously occurred to me that our father's use of his parental authority over us had been abusive. However, I could now see quite clearly the evidence of it in my past behaviour and that of my siblings. Like me, my sister seemed to find no lasting satisfaction in anything, which produced an almost annual change of address and also several marriages.

My brother has always been popular and good fun to be with. But at home with the removal of his public mask, like his father before him his temper could be fiery and quick to ignite. His eldest daughter, it seemed, was usually the recipient of his temper. I had believed this was simply a family trait therefore had given it little thought. However, during this unique week I received revelation that my brother had carried a slumbering rage from childhood, a legacy of the verbal abuse he had suffered. When his small daughter spoke to him in an impertinent manner, it was not the voice of a child he heard, but the voice of his father berating him yet again. Subconsciously he was unable to separate her childish impudence from the words that had unwittingly been used to systematically demolish my brother's confidence and self-esteem in his own childhood. As a child, my brother had no control over what was said to him, but now he was quick to execute punishment on anyone who dared to speak to him in an inappropriate manner. It made me so sad to see him unconsciously inflict the same pain on his own children that had been inflicted upon him. He had so wanted to be a better parent to his own family than his father had been to him, but he instinctively continued the same behaviour he had learned by example.

I could not understand where all this knowledge came from, as new revelation came to me daily. It was as though a window had been opened into another dimension and through it poured unprecedented insight about my family. If it had not been for the prophetic words of Pastor David Carr at the dawn of the year, I would have thought I was losing my mind. I began to ask God why He was showing me all these things. As I waited in silence, from deep within my spirit came a still small voice telling me, "It's because I love you." I was suddenly aware of an indescribable sense of inner quiet, unlike anything I had ever known before; it was like the complete stillness that comes when the first snows of winter have fallen.

When later reading my Bible, I came across a scripture that read:

'Surely I have calmed and quieted my soul like a weaned child with his mother: Like a weaned child, is my soul within me.' Psalm 131: 2

Those words were a perfect description of how I felt. For the first time in my life my soul was quiet within me. I had been previously unaware of a continual jarring, like the noise a radio makes when not tuned into a station properly. Until it suddenly disappeared, I was unaware of its existence because it had accompanied me for so long. I instantly recognised it as the clamour for approval, to quiet my feelings of inadequacy. I also saw that Pastor David was correct in saying my faith had been immature. For although I knew God's love for me was not based on what I did, still I battled with a voice deep within that told me if I did better, God would love me more, now that voice was silenced. I felt as safe and secure in the love of my Heavenly Father as a baby in the arms of her mother. I no longer needed people's approval for I knew I had

God's and that was enough.

As the week came to an end so did the stream of remarkable revelations. However, while I was praying at the close of this unique week a final picture came to my mind. I saw a beautiful garden bursting with flowers. In the midst of the garden a large dandelion grew quite unnoticed, camouflaged by the colourful array of beautiful flowers surrounding it. In my vision I saw a hand reach down and very gently pull out the dandelion removing the entire root, leaving nothing behind. I knew God was telling me the garden was a picture of my life and every secret thing in it had finally been uncovered and removed. Then the window I had been allowed to look through for a brief moment was closed.

Chapter 22

"Oh death where is thy sting?!"

In the weeks that followed, my mother made a quite remarkable recovery from the Guillan-Barrie syndrome. However, our joy was short lived when we discovered she had not fully regained all of her faculties. The illness had taken away parts of her memory. Never again would she be able to cook, or sew (which had once been her passion), or even write her own name. She simply had no recollection of how to do these once familiar things.

During the month of August that year, one Sunday, Phil and I were attending church as usual. The pain of recent events was fading and the relationship with my father had once again been restored. I was so enjoying the melodious music and the worship that I was hardly aware of anyone around me. As I worshiped a thought dropped into my mind. I suddenly knew I was going to write a book to tell people how God can transform even the most wretched life beyond recognition, simply by that person putting their trust in Him. In that instant I knew that I had gone to Bible College all those years before, not primarily to study theology but to get a rounded education, for I had been quite resistant to any knowledge the teachers had tried to instil in me when I had been at school. I wept with elation for I realised this had been God's plan for me all along, 'for He knew the plans He had for me, they were plans for good and not for evil to give me a hope and a future.' Jeremiah 29:11.

In the weeks that followed I quite naïvely set about beginning the task that lay before me, little realising what it would demand, or how long it would take. However, in the days, months and even years that followed I proceeded towards my goal.

My mother never quite returned to her former self. As time went by it became increasingly evident that her mental health was deteriorating even further. As she slipped further and further away from reality, sadly it was my sister who bore the full burden. Living so close to our parents, my father called upon her day and night for help. Initially my mother's declining mental health was thought to be latent symptoms of the Guillan-Barrie syndrome. However a series of tests proved it was in fact Alzheimer's disease.

It was only a matter of months after the diagnosis that my mother was transferred to a nursing home, mainly due to my father's inability to cope with the increasingly demanding situation. I watched with sorrow my father's once robust health decline as he himself became increasingly depressed and frail, wracked by loneliness and guilt that he could not cope with my mother's irrational behaviour. It seemed I hardly ever visited my father without seeing him descend into floods of tears.

When he himself was finally admitted to hospital for an operation to remove gallstones he gave the medical staff reason for concern when he later flatly refused to allow them to proceed with medical intervention due to his confused state of mind. I was at home preparing to visit him when I received a phone call telling me to go to the hospital immediately, for he had taken a turn for the worse. Only days before my father had enjoyed going around the beds chatting to the other patients, so this news came as a shock.

Due to the urgency in the voice of the caller I promptly contacted my sister to arrange to meet her at the hospital. As my brother was still the recipient of our father's wrath, I thought it was unwise to inform him of this latest turn of events, for I knew it would make my father angry to see him.

When Gail and I saw our father he was conscious and quite coherent. Nevertheless, we were invited to an interview with the Registrar who told us our father had developed peritonitis. We were told an operation would be performed if we wished, although little hope was given of recovery. Because he had also previously adamantly refused an operation we both felt we could not go against the desires he had so vehemently voiced.

By late afternoon, with the aid of sedatives and painkillers, my father had slipped into unconsciousness. My sister and I continued to sit on either side of his bed until nearly midnight hoping to see a last spark of life, but in reality waiting for his final breath. Although we had earlier been invited to stay, through sheer fatigue we decided to wait at home for the final phone call.

When I got home I collapsed into bed, surprised at how just sitting for several hours had completely sapped my energy. However, I slept very little and by five am sleep had completely deserted me, so on a cold, dark November morning I drove back to the hospital. Before the night staff went home they came to change the bedding in my father's private room. From outside the door I could hear the nurses talk to my unconscious father.

"Do you think he can hear you?" I asked, when they came out.

"How do you know he can't?" one replied.

So when I went back in, I sat very close to my father and quietly talked and sang to him. A short time later I turned round and was startled to find a different nurse had entered the room. Hearing me sing Christian songs to my father she asked if I required a Priest or a clergyman.

"What for?" I enquired.

"Oh, some people do at times like this." She said.

I explained that I was a committed Christian so it wasn't necessary. At this time in the morning and under these conditions I had no desire to enter into conversation with this excessively jovial nurse. Nevertheless, she blithely continued to tell me how her father, reaching a critical time in his own illness, happily entertained a minister of any denomination or religion whatsoever, although he had no personal faith of his own. "I told him, you're hedging your bets!" she laughed, "Well, they're all the same, aren't they?" she added.

I didn't answer immediately but pondered on her words for a minute or two, before replying rather more sharply than I had intended. "Actually they are not all the same! All roads do not lead to Rome; neither do all roads lead to Heaven. It says in the Bible, 'There is no other name under Heaven by which we must be saved, except the name of Jesus'. (Acts: 4:12.) Jesus himself said, 'I am the Way, the Truth, and the Life. No man comes to the Father except through me.' (John 14:6) So no, I don't agree with you, all religions are not the same!" With that I turned to my father. When I turned round again she had gone.

In the soft shadowy glow of the hospital nightlight I gazed into my father's face, knowing this would be his last day on earth. As I held his hand to my cheek, tears began to trickle down my face. Eventually the trickle grew to a flood until I could not stop crying. I wondered why I was weeping so profusely at the passing of this man who had caused me so much pain throughout much of my life. Not only did I sob uncontrollably, but groaned deeply in the Spirit as I prayed in the heavenly language God had given me so long ago.

As I leaned over my father to kiss his face, I was suddenly engulfed in an embrace so strong that it almost took my breath away. That my father had gathered his last remaining strength to hug me melted my heart; thereafter I made no attempt to halt my tears.

My sister arrived about 10.30am looking drained and tired. For most of the time we sat in silence on either side of our father's bed, each holding one of his hands. I felt faintly uncomfortable to be the one weeping at his bedside, for we both knew until only relatively recently it was she who had enjoyed a special place in his affections. I was the one renowned for being able, with very little effort, to put him in a rage within a matter of minutes. I made a feeble attempt to restrain my tears, but with little success. Defensively I said quietly, "This should be you."

"I know," she agreed. Then the room fell silent again as we each returned to our own thoughts. At around 3pm through sheer exhaustion, I decided to go home for a nap. My sister said she would do the same when I returned to the hospital later. I wearily crawled into bed that dark afternoon and instantly fell asleep, awakened only a short time later by the telephone ringing. I picked up the receiver to hear my sister tell me, "He's gone."

As I slowly emerged from sleep just before dawn the next day I heard the whisper of God speak to me within my spirit. He told me the conversation I had had with the nurse in my father's room had been for my father's benefit not hers, for he could hear every word. My tears at his bedside and the prayers that seemed to come from the very depth of my being that day was battling for my father's lost soul. The hug he succeeded in giving me with his last remaining strength was to say "goodbye" and to let me know that he finally believed.

Although my father left nothing to me of material value, that final gesture was priceless for I knew my father had made it to heaven. Sadly he had rejected the Lord for most of his life; he could have known such joy had he believed earlier.

I smiled every time I thought of my father in the days that followed, for I could only imagine the look of wonder on his face when he stepped into the glories of heaven.

It was only four months after the death of my father that I received an urgent telephone call from the care home where my mother lived. Being gravely ill already, I was told it was unlikely she would be able to fight off this latest chest infection. Not knowing how I would find her I took my Bible with me.

My mother had already slipped into unconsciousness by the time I arrived. Again, it was only my sister and I that sat at her bedside; however neither Gail nor I had any tears for our mother for we had been mourning her loss for several years already. Although my mother had always been very slim she now looked so emaciated I hardly recognised the person she had once been, for she had almost stopped eating completely due to the Alzheimer's disease. Each time I saw her, a little more of the person I had once known had disappeared, until there was hardly anything left of my mum.

As I sat at her bedside, periodically I read to her from the Bible. At one point I read that familiar scripture, Psalm 23. 'The Lord is my shepherd, I shall not want'. As I did I saw the trace of a smile steal across her face. I knew somewhere in the depths of my mother's shattered mind she had heard and had been encouraged by The Word of God. It was only a few hours later that my mother took her last breath.

•   •   •   •

It has now been several years since my parents died. If you are reading this you will know that I completed the assignment to write my book. Both my siblings have become grandparents. Although I don't see my sister as often as I would like, my brother and I still live close to each other and remain good friends. After over thirty years of marriage Phil and I are still happy together and still make each other laugh. Amazingly I enjoyed the same job in a local hospital where I worked as a ward receptionist for many years until I retired. Our daughter is currently a teaching assistant in a school for children with behavioural problems. I proudly stand back in amazement at the beautiful Godly woman she has grown into.

Dear reader, the purpose of this book is that what you have read may cause you to know that as God did with Adam of old He can still take a common piece of clay, breathe His Life into it and then polish that person until they become a diamond. He puts impossible dreams into the heart of that believer, in order to see their joy when He brings those dreams to pass. This is what happened to me and I thank God this is not the end of the story, there is still more to come.

I am just one of the myriad of people down through the ages, across the planet, who has dared to believe God's Word. In so doing they have seen the miraculous unfold before their very eyes.

Sandie George 2012

I WILL RISE AND STAND
AND TELL THIS LAND
WHAT THE GOOD LORD HAS DONE FOR ME

If you have been inspired by this story and you too would like God in your life, pray:

Heavenly Father,

I believe that you sent your son Jesus to pay for the sins of the world when He died and rose again.
Today I want to invite You in to my life and receive You into all that I have and am.

Thank you Lord.

(Ask God to direct you to a church that believes the Bible).

Sandie can be contacted at:

riseandstand@hotmail.co.uk